John C.

Answers to the

most commonly

asked questions

about Microsoft®

Windows NT™—

from concepts

through planning

and installation.

TM

Microsoft
PRESS
®

WINDOWS NT™

WINDOWS NT™

ANSWER BOOK

WINDOWS NT™

ANSWER BOOK

JIM GROVES

WITH A FOREWORD BY PAUL MARITZ

PUBLISHED BY
Microsoft Press
A Division of Microsoft Corporation
One Microsoft Way
Redmond, Washington 98052-6399

Library of Congress Cataloging-in-Publication Data
Groves, James A., 1953–
    Windows NT answer book / James A. Groves.
       p.   cm.
    Includes index.
    ISBN 1-55615-562-X
    1.   Operating systems (Computers)   2. Windows NT.   I. Title.
QA76.76.O63G773 1993
005.4'469--dc20   93-510
                                                            CIP

Printed and bound in the United States of America.

1 2 3 4 5 6 7 8 9 AG–M 8 7 6 5 4 3

Distributed to the book trade in Canada by Macmillan of Canada, a division of Canada Publishing
Corporation.

Distributed to the book trade outside the United States and Canada by Penguin Books Ltd.

Penguin Books Ltd., Harmondsworth, Middlesex, England
Penguin Books Australia Ltd., Ringwood, Victoria, Australia
Penguin Books N.Z. Ltd., 182-190 Wairau Road, Auckland 10, New Zealand

British Cataloging-in-Publication Data available.

Acquisitions Editor: J. F. Brown
Project Editor: Casey D. Doyle
Technical Reviewer: David Rygmyr

To Patty, who deserves this more than anyone else, despite what she thinks.

Contents

Part 3   Using Windows NT Networking Features

Appendixes

Foreword

Microsoft Windows NT is an important operating system for the computer industry. It has been designed specifically to solve a dilemma that has confronted corporate computer users for some time: Should they invest in PCs, with their ready appeal to the end user and an extraordinarily wide choice of hardware and software suppliers, or should they invest in minicomputer and mainframe systems that—despite their greater functionality, robustness, security, and scalability—are hard to use and offer comparatively few choices in hardware and software?

Windows NT represents a synthesis of the best of PC computing, minicomputer and mainframe computing, and network computing. Windows NT presents a foundation upon which organizations can build for many years to come, allowing new generations of hardware to be supported while preserving customers' present investments in software. Windows NT provides companies and government agencies the opportunity to integrate the currently separate "worlds of computing" within their organizations while achieving better results and lower costs.

Such a synthesis is not easy. In fact, it is the result only of careful design and years of development. In its first release, Windows NT can

- Run existing MS-DOS–based and Microsoft Windows–based software
- Run at high levels of performance
- Run on computers from a variety of manufacturers, including machines based on the Intel line of microprocessors and on RISC-based microprocessors
- Run on single-processor and multiprocessor machines
- Run as both a network client and server
- Support new classes of 32-bit programs
- Be certifiable as secure by government agencies

Because it integrates these features, Windows NT represents a huge technical achievement—the product of a group of some 300 persons of diverse skills and backgrounds who have worked as a team for more than four years. Windows NT comprises more than 3.5 million new lines of computer code, which, if printed out, would fill a small library—yet each of these lines must be correct. In fact, even more code had to be written simply to check the system and guarantee its solidity, followed by years of testing, analysis, corrections, and retesting. Even beyond that, Windows NT's functioning has been documented with a clarity that provides not only an overview of the system but also describes its countless details.

Windows NT represents an enormous endeavor and stands as a testament to the tireless dedication and iron self-discipline of the team that produced it.

Paul Maritz
Senior Vice President, Systems Division
Microsoft Corporation

Preface

In the more than four years that I have been a technical writer at Microsoft, I have never seen an impending software release generate as much widespread anticipation as the Microsoft Windows NT operating system. I've also never seen a more public software development project at Microsoft. Most products in development are given code names (at one point Windows for Workgroups was known as Winball, for instance), and insiders are cautioned not to talk to anyone about their projects, even merely to acknowledge their existence.

Windows NT, on the other hand, has always been wide open to the world. Microsoft has talked about it openly to the press and has demonstrated it to thousands of people, distributing prerelease versions to many of them (most of whom are software developers and large corporate users) to install and try out on their own computers, all without the restrictions of the usual "nondisclosure agreement" designed to keep a new product secret. Windows NT has been named a "Best Buy for 1993" by *Corporate Computing* magazine (even before Windows NT's release) and has been written about extensively by general-interest news and business publications.

Because of this publicity, a great deal of curiosity has existed about Windows NT, not only among "computer professionals," but also among those who simply use computers as part of their daily routine but who don't tend to think of themselves as computer experts.

For those of you who fit into the latter category, I wrote *Windows NT Answer Book* with you in mind. If you're shaking your head and thinking of putting this book back on the shelf because you don't know what all the terms inside this book mean, that's good. It means you have the right book if you want to learn about Windows NT. If you already know the terms, this book is for you too.

If you've already leafed through the rest of this book, you've probably noticed that it doesn't look like most other books about computers. I've tried to make this book as easy for you to browse through as possible. To do this, I've forced myself to try to write about one subject at a time and to limit myself to two pages about that one topic (and believe me, it's harder than it sounds). Also, because I figured you'd be reading this book to answer your own questions about Windows NT, I've tried to anticipate your questions and have set out to answer them. That's why every even-numbered page begins with a question I hope you might ask. Following each question is a brief answer appearing in italics. If the brief answer is enough to answer the question adequately, you can move on to the next question (whichever one you happen to turn to next). If you need more information, you can read the longer answer that fills out the remainder of the two-page spread.

Feel free to read *Windows NT Answer Book* however you want—you don't need to feel somehow "honor bound" to read it from cover to cover. Instead, leaf through it. Find a question that strikes your fancy and read the answer. Unavoidably, in some instances you'll find that the answer assumes you understand something that was introduced earlier in the book. (Although I've tried to avoid these situations, sometimes it's impossible to add all the necessary context in one place without recapping the entire book up to that point.) In that case, use the table of contents to look for a question earlier in the book that you think might be pertinent, or use the index to search for the topic you have in mind.

Another way *Windows NT Answer Book* differs from most computer books is in its basic purpose. Most books about operating systems and applications are oriented toward telling you step by step how to take specific actions. In this book, however, you won't find pictures of dialog boxes or lists of procedures to follow. Instead, *Windows NT Answer Book* is designed to teach you the general concepts you need to use Windows NT if you're already familiar with Windows. Once you understand these concepts, you'll probably be able to apply them with little additional help. If you do need assistance, the printed and online documentation that accompanies Windows NT will also help to meet your needs.

If you opened this book expecting a more advanced discussion on the technical details of Windows NT, I'm sorry to disappoint you. I can, however, strongly recommend that you read *Inside Windows NT*, by Helen Custer, also published by Microsoft Press. *Inside Windows NT* exhaustively details the design philosophy and inner workings of Windows NT. Despite its esoteric subject matter, it is surprisingly readable and quite interesting.

Like Helen, I was able to write my book about Windows NT as a Microsoft insider. I belong to the Windows NT User Education team, which has been hard at work readying the user manuals and online help for Windows NT. I am grateful for the opportunity I've had to draw upon the expertise and insights of my coworkers during the preparation of this book. That my name can be attached to this book while they labor anonymously is truly an injustice. It certainly should not be construed as a judgment of the relative merit of our respective accomplishments. *Windows NT Answer Book* can exist in its present form only because of the support their manuals and online help provide to those who use Windows NT.

I think it also important to recognize the contribution made by the many people in Windows NT program management, development, and product management who took time to supply information used in this book and to review it for accuracy and completeness. Particularly as the deadline to "ship" it has drawn near, time becomes an extremely rare commodity, and I am grateful for their effort to share some of it with me. Despite our best efforts, however, no doubt I have allowed errors and omissions to remain, and since I am their author, I accept sole responsibility for the inaccuracies.

I am especially grateful to the staff of Microsoft Press for their patience and responsiveness as together we have struggled to turn this book from a manual that was destined for the box into a book that's suitable for the shelf. I am especially indebted to my editor, Casey Doyle, for his thorough yet judicious editing. This book would be far less readable were it not for his well-tempered pencil.

Finally, I want to leave you with one minor thought. *Windows NT Answer Book* was committed to the printing press before Windows NT itself was officially completed. As a result, changes might have occurred in the operating system by the time you read this book. But I'm confident that the conceptual material is solid and valuable, transcending any minutiae regarding changes to the operating system.

And now, let us begin our exchange of questions and answers with that query that most likely is at the top of your list: "What is Microsoft Windows NT?" I hope you like what you read.

Jim Groves
March 1993

PART 1

Introducing the Microsoft
Windows NT Operating System

What is Microsoft Windows NT?

Microsoft Windows NT is the newest and most powerful member of the Microsoft Windows family of operating systems. Although it is a completely new operating system capable of taking full advantage of a broad range of highly advanced computer hardware, Windows NT retains the familiarity and ease of use of Microsoft Windows 3.1. Windows NT features built-in security and networking, and is available in versions for workstations and for servers.

Today's smaller personal computers are, by most measures, more powerful than their massive cousins of only a few years ago. The number of computations personal computers (sometimes called "PCs") can perform each second, the amount of memory they have available to store running applications and their data, and the sophistication of the interaction between personal computers and their users have all improved at a breathtaking pace every year.

Microsoft MS-DOS and Microsoft Windows have been important parts of this process. MS-DOS is, by far, the most widely used computer operating system ever developed. By providing a standard operating system for personal computers built by many different manufacturers, MS-DOS has played a crucial role in the third-party development of thousands of different applications that can all run on MS-DOS–based computers.

Since 1990, when Microsoft released Windows version 3.0, Windows has become the new operating system standard for computers based on the Intel 80386 and 80486 microprocessors. Microsoft Windows not only adds a graphical user interface to MS-DOS–based computers, it also extends MS-DOS itself to provide basic *multitasking* (the ability to run more than one application at a time) and improved memory management. These features of Windows, coupled with its facility for *application integration* (the ability of applications to share information with each other through facilities of the operating system), make MS-DOS–based personal computers easier to use now than at any time in the past.

Subsequent releases of Windows added to its success, particularly as new features were added to extend its usefulness on many different types of computers. Most recently, Windows for Workgroups makes it easy to link computers in networks so that they (and their users) can communicate with each other.

Windows NT continues this process of evolution and innovation by adding the power and scalability of an advanced operating system to the ease-of-use and application benefits that are already a part of Windows on many of the most powerful single-user computers available. Windows NT does this by breaking the link between Windows and MS-DOS, thereby making it possible to run Windows NT without MS-DOS on computers based on the Intel 80x86 family of microprocessors as well as on computers based on microprocessors outside the Intel 80x86 family.

This characteristic of Windows NT (known as *portability*) means that Windows NT can be readily adapted to run on virtually any computer with a 32-bit microprocessor, helping to ensure that it will be able to take advantage of future advances in hardware technology from many different manufacturers. A byproduct of this portability is *scalability*, the ability to adjust the operating system to a broad range of hardware platforms. Because Windows NT is scalable, computer manufacturers can alter it to run on systems built with 2 to 32 microprocessors in addition to common single-microprocessor systems.

Because today's personal computers are so powerful, Windows NT includes features that would have overwhelmed early PCs. One of these features is integrated security. Windows NT security makes it easy to control who can use the computer and the type of access each user is allowed to the computer's resources. Windows NT security can also provide protection against computer viruses and other maliciously designed programs that might otherwise damage the computer or its data.

Windows NT provides extensive support for connecting computers to form a network, allowing them to communicate and share resources. Every computer running Windows NT can make resources such as files and printers available to other computers on a network. Also, Windows NT gives users the familiar Windows user interface, thus making it easier to manage the computers on the network.

To meet the needs of larger networks, an extended version of Windows NT, the Microsoft Windows NT Advanced Server, provides additional capabilities that further simplify network management and makes the operation of servers more reliable.

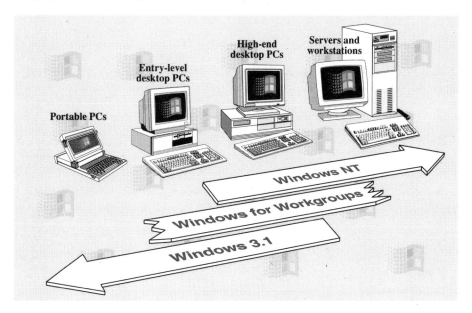

How does Windows NT compare with Windows 3.1?

Windows NT brings the power and ease-of-use of the Windows family of operating systems to high-end computers. Windows NT has all the capabilities of Windows 3.1 and adds the ability to handle more system resources and other benefits of a high-end operating system. Windows NT is designed to complement Windows 3.1, not replace it.

For users of Windows 3.1, one of the most significant features of Windows NT is that it *is* Windows. The familiar features of Windows 3.1's *user interface* are nearly identical in Windows NT. For example, Program Manager, File Manager, Print Manager, and the Control Panel are essentially the same, except where changes were required to support Windows NT's advanced features.

More importantly, Windows NT runs nearly all Windows 3.1–based applications and newer applications developed to take advantage of Windows NT's unique features with full support for object linking and embedding (OLE) and dynamic data exchange (DDE) among them. Experienced developers of Windows 3.1–based applications will be immediately productive in developing applications for Windows NT because Windows NT uses the same development environment used by Windows 3.1.

Although Windows 3.1 and Windows NT appear very similar to the user, they are very different under the surface. This difference makes each operating system better suited for certain uses.

Windows 3.1 works with MS-DOS and continues to rely on MS-DOS for some of its basic functions, which allows Windows 3.1 to run on computers that do not have the capacity to support a high-end operating system such as Windows NT. Most people who use personal computers run personal-productivity applications—that is, applications intended to help individual users do their work. Windows 3.1 is especially well suited for these kinds of applications.

Windows NT is a completely new operating system that is not built on MS-DOS. This design makes it possible to adapt Windows NT to run on a wide range of high-end computer systems, including computers based on new microprocessor designs and computers with multiple microprocessors, that cannot run Windows 3.1.

In addition to being able to run on other types of high-end computers, Windows NT adds unique features to the Windows family that make Windows NT an especially powerful platform for running mission-critical applications—applications that require a reliable and responsive operating system. Included in these features are complete memory protection, a powerful and reliable file system, and security and network support built into every part of the operating system.

A characteristic that mission-critical applications usually have in common is a need for large amounts of memory that cannot be corrupted by other application programs. Windows NT can provide up to 2 gigabytes (GB) of memory to each application, and this memory is completely protected by the operating system to ensure that no application (or Windows NT itself) can be affected by an error in another application's programming.

Another feature that Windows NT brings to the Windows family is security: Windows NT lets you control who can use your computer and how it can be used. Taking advantage of Windows NT's security means that you can be sure that your organization's critical data is available to those people (and only to those people) who need it.

Flexible and reliable data storage is also a common requirement for mission-critical applications. The Windows NT file system (NTFS) provides fast file-system recovery in case of computer failure. NTFS also supports long filenames, integrated security, and the ability to exploit a virtually unlimited disk size.

By extending the Windows family to high-end computers, Windows NT makes it possible to make Windows the standard platform throughout an organization. On a network, for example, most users can run Windows for Workgroups and their personal-productivity applications. High-performance systems can run Windows NT as the platform for an enterprise's mission-critical applications as well as for personal-productivity applications. Because Windows NT, Windows for Workgroups, and Windows 3.1 share the same user interface, applications, and programming interface, users and application developers can move among computers running these operating systems with ease—many, in fact, might not even be aware (or care) that the computers are not running the same operating system.

How does Windows NT make my system easier to use?

Windows NT brings the power and ease of use of Microsoft Windows to a broad range of advanced computer systems, extending the availability of Microsoft Windows to computers ranging from laptop computers to closet-sized network servers. As a result, users can control their computers and run the same applications the same way, whether they are using a standard PC or a powerful RISC-based workstation.

One of the reasons many people think computers are hard to use is that early computers *were* difficult to use. The limited capabilities of these computers required a relatively unsophisticated means of controlling them. Most often this meant that the operating system provided some type of arcane command language with which the user controlled the computer. Users were expected to master dozens of different commands, each with its own syntax, to perform even the simplest functions.

The emergence of the graphical user interface has radically changed the way people use computers, making the computer look and work in a way most people find more natural than the method provided by command languages. For example, with the graphical user interface, to copy a file to a floppy disk a user can simply drag an on-screen icon representing the file to an icon representing a floppy disk drive.

Another important benefit of a graphical user interface is the opportunity it provides to establish a common user interface between all the applications designed for it. Application programmers can draw upon a single graphical user interface to give users a consistent way to work with different applications. For instance, the menus of different applications tend to contain many of the same commands (such as File Open). Even for commands unique to a specific application, the menus of which they are a part work the same way as they do in other applications. Many users find that the more applications they learn for a particular graphical user interface, the easier it is to use new applications for that same interface.

Below the surface, the Windows user interface provides facilities for *application integration,* giving different applications the ability to easily exchange information. Microsoft Windows, for example, provides *dynamic data exchange* (DDE), a method that a Windows-based application can use to communicate directly with any other Windows-based application. Windows also provides for *object linking and embedding* (OLE), which gives a Windows-based application the ability to incorporate information from any other Windows-based application, even if the two applications are not designed to work specifically with each other.

Microsoft Windows is the most widely used graphical user interface in the world. Millions of people rely on its visual methods for accessing their computers' resources and working with Windows-based applications. Because of this popularity, many thousands of applications have been written for the Windows user interface. Until Windows NT, however, Windows could run only on computers using MS-DOS. This meant that Windows-based applications could not run on other types of computers, such as workstations based on reduced instruction set computing (RISC) microprocessors.

For the first time, Windows NT brings the ease of use and consistency of Windows to computers that do not run MS-DOS. This means that users can run the same Windows-based applications on computers ranging from laptops running Windows 3.1 to multiprocessor workstations running Windows NT, and these applications will look and work the same on all these computers.

The consistency provided by Windows running on many different platforms can significantly reduce training costs and boost user productivity. An individual can work the same way, whether using a laptop or a workstation, without having to learn to manage each computer and its applications separately.

The availability of the same user interface and application environment on different types of computers also makes managing mixed computer installations easier. Those who are responsible for supporting computer users in an organization interact with the same user interface and application software on all computers. For example, the process necessary to set up a word processing application is the same for all computers when they all have the same user interface. This is not true when computers are running different user interfaces with separate methods for installing application software.

Perhaps the most important benefit of Windows' scalability, however, is the way it facilitates communication among computers, particularly on a network. Because computers running a member of the Windows operating system family share a common method of transferring data, they can share information more easily than could computers running different operating systems.

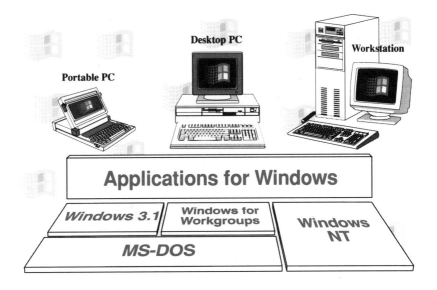

How does Windows NT allow me to run more kinds of applications?

Applications are generally designed to work with one operating system. Windows NT, however, not only runs 32-bit applications created specifically for Windows NT, but also runs 16-bit applications created for Windows 3.1, MS-DOS, and OS/2 1.x character mode, as well as applications that meet the POSIX standard. Windows NT is the only operating system that can run applications created for all of these application environments.

An essential attribute of an operating system concerns the applications it can run. Chances are slim that you would choose an operating system for a particular computer without first taking into account the type of work to be done with the computer and the applications that would best support that work.

Every operating system provides a way for applications to request services from the operating system. This is generally known as the operating system's *application programming interface*, or API. A programmer writing an application to run on a particular operating system calls upon the parts of the operating system's API that make the desired operating system services available to the application. For example, a programmer who wants the application to create a file will write the program so that it calls upon that portion of the operating system's API that manages files.

The principal API for Windows NT is the 32-bit Microsoft Win32 API. The Win32 API provides all the necessary connections between an application and the Windows NT operating system. An application must be created to conform with the Win32 API to take full advantage of the capabilities of Windows NT.

Most often, an operating system is capable of running only applications created to conform to the operating system's own API. This is not the case with Windows NT, however. Instead, Windows NT can run applications created to conform to the API of any of several operating systems, including Windows 3.1, MS-DOS, OS/2 1.x character mode, and POSIX-compliant operating systems. Windows does this by intercepting the API requests made by applications designed for these other operating systems and translating them into their Win32 equivalents. In effect, Windows NT emulates the operating system necessary to run the application, responding to the application's service requests just as its intended operating system would.

Windows NT handles applications that must have direct access to the computer's hardware in a similar way. Windows NT must mediate every application's attempt to access computer hardware to prevent applications from interfering with each other and with Windows NT itself. (This is also an important requirement of Windows NT's security.) To allow Windows NT to control applications that must have direct access to the computer's hardware, a virtual device driver is necessary. Windows NT contains virtual device drivers for the most commonly accessed devices (such as communications ports), and so many applications that access these devices will be able to run properly. If an application requires access to a custom device (such as a scanner interface), however, a virtual device driver developed by the device manufacturer might be required before the application can run on Windows NT.

Although these applications don't conform to Win32, they can run on Windows NT:

Windows 3.1–based applications

Applications written for Windows 3.1 use a combination of the Windows 3.1 API and the MS-DOS API. Because the Win32 API is an extension of the 16-bit Windows 3.1 API, Windows 3.1 applications can run on Windows NT without modification. Windows NT can run these applications not only on computers based on the Intel 80x86 family of microprocessors but also on RISC-based computers.

MS-DOS–based applications

More applications have been created for MS-DOS than for any other operating system. Windows NT can run these applications on computers based on the Intel 80x86 family of microprocessors and on RISC-based computers.

OS/2 1.x character-mode–based applications

Although far fewer applications conform to the 16-bit OS/2 1.x character-mode API than conform to the Windows 3.1 API or the MS-DOS API, these 16-bit OS/2 applications play an important role on some corporate networks, usually as server applications. By running these applications, Windows NT makes it easier to migrate from OS/2 to Windows NT.

POSIX-compliant applications

The Portable Operating System Interface (POSIX) standard was developed by the Institute of Electrical and Electronics Engineers (IEEE) to define an API for a standard set of operating system services. Applications that adhere to the POSIX standard, which is based on the UNIX operating system, can be easily moved from one POSIX-compliant operating system to another. Windows NT can run applications that comply with the IEEE POSIX.1 specification.

How does Windows NT use my computer's memory?

Windows NT is designed to exploit the benefits of modern 32-bit microprocessors. In addition to processing data more efficiently using 32-bit values, Windows NT takes advantage of the improved use of memory made possible by a 32-bit microprocessor, giving Windows NT access to as much as 4 gigabytes (GB) of memory. Windows NT also accesses hard disk storage using 64-bit addresses, allowing it access to practically unlimited hard disk space.

In recent years much has been made of the number of bits a computer system is designed to handle. Even video-game manufacturers have become involved, promoting their 16-bit systems as their latest and greatest offerings. Despite all the focus on the *number* of bits handled, however, little explanation is provided about why this is significant.

Simply put, a bit is a 0 or 1 value in the binary (also known as the base-2) number system. Because computers handle all computations and data in binary form, the number of bits a computer can handle at one time determines the largest number it can compute and, by extension, the amount of data it can access directly. Each byte in memory is identified by a number known as an *address*. The larger the number of addresses a microprocessor can handle, the more memory it can use.

MS-DOS and the first versions of Microsoft Windows were designed to run on computers based on the 16-bit Intel 8086 and 8088 microprocessors (or CPUs). The largest value that can be represented with 16 bits is 65,535 (because of rounding, commonly referred to as 64K), so the largest amount of memory that a 16-bit address can access directly is 64K. Because MS-DOS–based computers contain much more memory than 64K, this limitation was overcome by using a *segmented memory model*, a scheme in which multiple 64K chunks (called segments) exist, each of which has its own address. Because each byte in memory must be located using two addresses (one for the segment and one for the location of the byte within the segment), this requires extra computing steps, so the microprocessor is not used at peak efficiency. More importantly, it makes it more difficult for programs that require large amounts of memory to keep track of which segment contains a particular data item.

To get a rough idea of how the segmented memory of MS-DOS works, imagine that a 500-page book is bound into five 100-page volumes, each of which numbers its pages separately (that is, each begins with page 1). Because the 500-page book was arbitrarily divided into 100-page volumes, however, related information can continue from one volume to another. Thus, to read 15 pages of information beginning at page 96, you have to locate page 96 in Volume 1, read through page 100, set aside Volume I, take up Volume II, and continue reading at page 1 until you reach page 10.

More recent versions of MS-DOS and Windows are designed to work with newer 32-bit microprocessors (such as the Intel 80386 and 80486 microprocessors) and with memory-management software to make more memory available to applications. Even so, the requirement for MS-DOS to remain compatible with older, 16-bit micro-processors prevents these 32-bit operating system extensions from fully exploiting the capabilities of the 32-bit microprocessor.

Windows NT has been designed from the beginning with new programming code to fully employ the capabilities of 32-bit microprocessors. This allows Windows NT to use the microprocessor more efficiently, increasing overall system performance.

The most significant improvement that a fully 32-bit operating system provides is known as a *flat memory model*. A flat memory model (sometimes known as a *flat address space*) allows applications to use memory in an efficient manner. With Windows NT's flat memory model, memory is available as though it were arranged as one continuous list of bytes. The location (or address) of each byte is determined simply by how far it is from the top of the list. Drawing on our example of a book, the flat memory model is like a book bound in a single volume whose pages are numbered consecutively. To find information on pages 96 through 110, you simply turn to page 96 and read until you reach the end of page 110.

Windows NT can access up to 4 GB (that is, 4 billion bytes) of memory. Because of the way Windows NT uses *virtual memory* (hard disk space used to simulate memory) and manages memory on behalf of applications, each application can have access to as much as 2 GB of memory. (The total amount of memory actually available depends on how much RAM is installed in the computer.)

Windows NT goes a step further, however, with hard disk space. Instead of using 32-bit values for the addresses it uses to access hard disk space, Windows NT uses 64-bit values. (Windows NT uses addresses to identify locations on a hard disk much as it does locations in memory.) This enables Windows NT to access a vast amount of space on each partition: about 16 billion GB (the square of 4 GB).

What are the benefits of Windows NT's task-management features?

Like other modern operating systems, Windows NT can run more than one application at the same time. In addition, applications created for Windows NT can be divided into threads that can run simultaneously, further improving performance, especially on systems with more than one microprocessor. Windows NT always retains control of the system microprocessor—no application can seize control of the microprocessor or the computer's input devices.

The ability of a computer to run more than one application at a time is not new. This ability first became available in the early 1960s on large mainframe computers that supported several users simultaneously accessing the computer through separate terminals. In effect, each user ran a different application with the operating system, which gave each application a share of the computer's time. Such setups came to be known as *time-sharing systems*.

The first personal computers were designed to be used by a single user, so the need to run multiple applications simultaneously was not obvious. Consequently, the first operating systems for personal computers were capable of running only one application at a time.

Before long the restrictions and inconvenience this imposed became apparent, so methods were developed that allowed the computer to simulate doing two operations at once. One popular method was to use terminate-and-stay-resident (TSR) applications that would sit idle in memory until called upon, usually by a particular keystroke. The TSR application would take control of the computer until dismissed, and then would return control to the application that was running when the TSR was summoned.

The development of the graphical user interface (GUI) of window-oriented operating systems such as Microsoft Windows provided the ability to run more than one application at the same time, a capability commonly known as *multitasking*. (Time-sharing is running multiple applications on behalf of multiple users; multitasking is usually used to mean running multiple applications on behalf of a single user.) Windows 3.1 is based on a system known as *cooperative multitasking* because Windows-based applications must cooperate with each other so that each can be given its share of the microprocessor's time. In other words, each application must yield control of the system before another can gain it.

The chief problem of this system is that a given application might not cooperate, interfering with the ability of other applications to operate properly. For example, a poorly designed application can fail to yield control when it is in the process of sorting a list of items in memory. Even worse, some application errors can cause the application to lock up: Because the operating system is waiting for the application to yield control, the entire computer is effectively disabled.

In contrast to cooperative multitasking, Windows NT provides *preemptive multitasking*, in which the operating system preempts each application's control of the microprocessor. In effect, the operating system seizes control of the computer instead of waiting for an application to yield it. This helps to ensure that each running application is given its fair share of microprocessor time, allowing each to run simultaneously without interfering with any of the others.

A further enhancement to performance provided by Windows NT is its ability to execute multiple *threads* within a single application. This allows an application programmer to divide an application into several sections (called *threads*) that can run simultaneously. That way an application can perform tasks in the background (such as recalculating a large spreadsheet or printing a document) while continuing to allow the user to do other work with the application.

For example, a simple application that receives input, processes data, and prints reports but is not designed to use execution threads might work as shown in the illustration on the left:

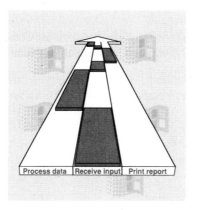 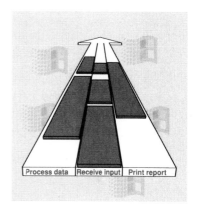

The bars shown in the illustration on the left do not overlap, indicating that the application can do only one operation at a time. In contrast, a similar application designed with multiple threads might work as shown in the illustration on the right: The overlapping bars indicate that more than one operation is happening at the same time, and as a result the overall process is shorter because the user doesn't have to wait for the completion of one task before starting another.

Performance increases dramatically when Windows NT runs on computers with more than one microprocessor. Through a process known as *symmetric multiprocessing*, Windows NT can use each microprocessor to run threads from the same application or from different applications (including the operating system itself), scheduling each thread to provide maximum system response.

How does Windows NT make my system more reliable?

Windows NT strictly controls how applications access your computer's memory and hardware. This ensures that no application can interfere with any other application or with the operating system itself. In addition, the advanced file system of Windows NT has fault-tolerance features that help avoid the corruption of data stored on your computer's hard disk.

One of the persistent problems with multitasking operating systems results when a badly designed application attempts to use memory that has been set aside for another application. Typically this causes both applications to fail and can even crash the entire system.

This situation typically occurs because multitasking operating systems allocate a block of system memory when an application requests it, but do not monitor how the application proceeds to use the memory.

For example, suppose the operating system allocates two blocks of memory, one for each of the two applications:

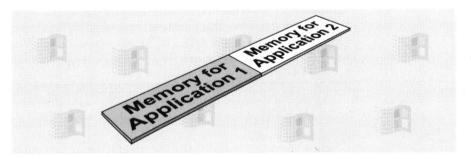

If Application 1 tries to use more memory than its allocation, however, the following results:

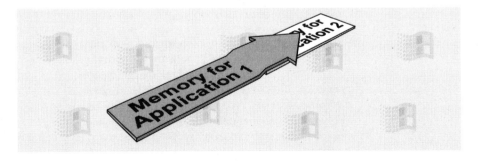

The result is either that the memory used by Application 2 becomes corrupted, or that Application 1 finds data that it is not prepared to handle. In this situation, chances are that one or both applications can no longer run properly.

Windows NT ensures that an application cannot access memory that the operating system has allocated to another application. If an application attempts to do so, Windows NT forces it to terminate so that one application cannot corrupt the memory belonging to the other application. Not only does this help preserve the integrity and reliability of applications, but it also ensures that no application can disable the operating system itself. Application errors can affect only the application containing the error, not other applications or the system as a whole. (Note, however, that Windows 3.1–based applications *rely* on being able to access a common pool of memory. Because Windows NT provides an emulated Windows 3.1 native environment, Windows 3.1–based applications running on Windows NT can interfere with each other's memory. They cannot affect other types of applications or Windows NT itself, however.)

In a similar fashion, Windows NT does not allow applications to directly access the computer's hardware. Instead, Windows NT mediates all access to physical devices on behalf of applications. This prevents applications from interfering with each other (or with the operating system) as they attempt to use these devices. This is essential not only to improve reliability but to ensure system security.

Finally, Windows NT enhances your system's reliability through the advanced capabilities of the Windows NT file system (NTFS). NTFS incorporates features that make it *fault tolerant*—that is, able to continue operating reliably despite faults that produce hardware failures. NTFS maintains a transaction log that ensures the integrity of the hard disk structure even if the system fails unexpectedly.

For the particularly demanding requirements of a network server, the extended version of Windows NT known as Windows NT Advanced Server contains additional features that provide even greater fault tolerance, including *disk mirroring* and *disk striping*.

With disk mirroring, Windows NT Advanced Server continuously maintains a copy of the hard disk on another hard disk. In effect, the second hard disk acts as a backup to the first hard disk. Disk mirroring is more reliable and provides better performance if the hard disks are on drives with separate controllers, a disk-mirroring arrangement sometimes known as *disk duplexing*.

When implemented in a form known as *disk striping with parity,* disk striping lets you use multiple hard disks to improve the performance and reliability of hard disk storage. Disk striping creates several logical (named) disks, but instead of confining each logical disk to one physical disk drive, it spreads the logical disk's data across several separate hard disks. By itself, this decreases the amount of time required to read or record data, but it does not add to the logical disk's reliability. When disk striping is implemented with parity, however, additional data is recorded that allows the data contained in a faulty physical hard disk drive to be recovered.

How does integrated networking make using a network easier?

The ability to access and control a network is an integral feature of Windows NT. Every Windows NT workstation can share files, printers, and other resources with other computers on the network. The tools for using and controlling the network are built into the Windows NT user interface, making the network as easy to use as any other part of the system. In addition, Windows NT Advanced Server provides networking features that provide even greater reliability and easier network management.

As personal computers become more widespread within an organization, making the data stored on one computer available to other computers becomes increasingly difficult. It also becomes more difficult to give computer users convenient access to expensive peripherals such as printers.

Linking computers together to form a local area network (LAN) provides the solution to these needs and provides additional benefits as well. A simple LAN consists of two or more computers connected by network interface cards and cables in a relatively limited area (such as an office building). This setup allows them to communicate with each other directly so that they can share data and other resources.

The earliest operating systems for personal computers were developed before the importance of networks became apparent. As a result, these operating systems did little to make it easy to include a computer in a network.

Windows NT, on the other hand, has been designed from the beginning to provide full network support. The facilities for accessing and controlling the network are built into the same utilities used for managing the rest of the operating system, making it as easy to use the network as any other part of the computer. In other words, the network is an integral part of the operating system, not an afterthought or add-on.

The following provides a brief summary of many of the built-in networking features of Windows NT:

- Sharing files

  A Windows NT–based computer can make the files in any directory available to other computers on the network by sharing that directory. Sharing files is as simple as selecting the directory in File Manager and clicking a button. Any other computer on the network can then connect to the shared directory and use its files just as though the files were located on the other computer's own hard disk. Access to the files in the shared directory by other computers can be controlled by means of Windows NT's integrated security.

- Sharing printers

  A printer connected to a single computer is rarely kept busy all the time. A Windows NT–based computer can make one or more of its printers available to other computers on the network so that the other computers can use a printer just as if the printer were connected directly to each of the other computers. Sharing a printer on the network is as simple as selecting a printer with Print Manager and clicking a button.

- Exchanging electronic mail

  Windows NT includes Mail, a full-featured electronic mail (e-mail) application that lets users type messages, send them to other users on the network, and receive messages from other users. In addition to text, these messages can contain almost any kind of data that can be handled by the computer, such as pictures, spreadsheets, and even sound and video (on appropriately equipped computers).

- Maintaining group schedules

  In conjunction with Mail, Windows NT provides Schedule+, an application that maintains appointment schedules and task lists. Schedule+ can be of great help in scheduling a meeting with other people whose computers are also running Schedule+ and are connected to the network. The application can examine the other network users' schedules, show the times that the other users are available, and even use Mail to send an invitation to those who should attend.

- Running distributed applications

  Windows NT networking supports a *remote procedure call* (RPC) facility that gives specially developed applications the ability to communicate with applications running on other computers connected to the network. For example, a Windows NT application can use the RPC service to gather and consolidate information from databases maintained by several computers on the network. The Windows NT RPC facility complies with the Open Systems Foundation's Distributed Computing Environment (DCE) standard, ensuring that the Windows NT RPC service can communicate with servers running Windows NT, UNIX, VMS, and other DCE-compliant operating systems.

These network capabilities provide sufficient support for a small network. As such a network grows, however, it becomes increasingly difficult to manage because each computer on the network must be administered separately. In addition, the network quickly becomes essential to the day-to-day operation of the organization, so the reliability of the computers that share data becomes crucial.

An extended version of Windows NT known as Windows NT Advanced Server addresses the needs of a larger network. Windows NT Advanced Server organizes network computers in a domain. (A *domain* consists of a group of servers and workstations in an administrative unit.) The domain administrator can administer all the servers and workstations belonging to the domain over the network from a single computer. Also, a sufficiently equipped computer running Windows NT Advanced Server has additional fault-tolerance features (such as disk mirroring and disk striping with parity) that help ensure the availability and reliability of the data stored on that computer.

How can integrated security protect my system's data?

Windows NT lets you control who can use your computer and how they can use it. Users must identify themselves and supply their own, unique password. Once identified, a user must have permission to access various system resources, and each user can specify the type of access other users can have to resources under the user's control. In addition, only particular users are allowed to administer all or selected parts of the system.

One of the persistent problems of a personal computer running a conventional operating system is its accessibility: Anyone who can gain access to the keyboard and display is often capable of virtually unlimited control of the computer and the data it contains. Little can be done to prevent that person from looking at sensitive information, destroying essential data, or introducing a destructive computer virus.

Previously this risk was considered acceptable for most organizations because the personal computer was primarily a productivity tool not essential to the organization's primary function. Instead, essential business processes were handled by the organization's mainframe or midsize computer. Now, however, more and more organizations are engaged in a process called *downsizing,* transferring their line-of-business applications to network servers and workstations. As this happens, it becomes crucial to control access to those applications and to their data.

One of the principal design goals for Windows NT was to make it as secure as possible without significantly hindering its usability. As with networking, security has been designed into every aspect of the system from the beginning of the operating system's design, including its user interface. The result is that security is as easy to manage as any other part of the system.

Windows NT security protects the computer and its data by controlling who can use the computer, by limiting how someone can use it, and by monitoring how someone uses it.

Controlling who uses the computer

Windows NT protects the computer by allowing only authorized people to use it. To allow a person to access the computer, you create an account for that person. Only then can that person log on to the computer by supplying the name of the account and the matching secret password. Similarly, a user connecting to a shared resource on the computer over the network must also have an account on the computer and must supply the account's password before being allowed to use the resource.

Limiting how someone can use the computer

Even when authorized users log on to the computer, they do not have unlimited access to it. First, their authority to manage the computer is controlled by the operating system. This ensures that only specifically authorized users can manage critical parts of the system, particularly the system's security setup.

Second, a user can access only those resources (chiefly files and printers) for which the user has permission. Whoever owns the resource (typically the person who created the resource) can give or deny permission to other users for access to the resource, including the type of access permitted. For example, a user who creates a file can permit some users to read the file and allow other users to both read and change it. Users who do not have permission to access the file are not allowed to use the file at all.

Monitoring how someone uses the computer

Even the most carefully implemented security setup can have loopholes that an authorized user can pass through accidentally or on purpose. Monitoring how people are actually using the system is important to ensure that the system's security setup is working. For example, it is important to know whether there have been a large number of failed attempts to log on to the computer. That might indicate that someone is trying to break through the system's security.

Windows NT keeps a record of the security-related events that the computer's administrator chooses to monitor. The record can be used to determine whether a breach of security has occurred or simply to suggest where security measures might be tightened. The administrator can specify the types of events that are recorded, down to the level of file access by a particular user.

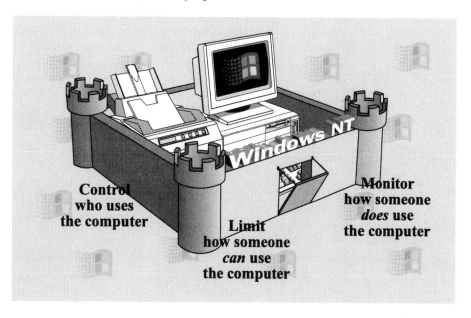

What kind of hardware do I need to run Windows NT?

Windows NT is designed to take advantage of the capabilities of advanced computer hardware. A typical Windows NT–based computer has an 80486-based or RISC-based microprocessor, 12 to 16 megabytes of memory, and a Super VGA display. The minimum requirements for Windows NT consist of a 25-MHz 80386 microprocessor, 8 megabytes of memory, and a VGA display.

As you might expect for such an advanced operating system, Windows NT's minimum hardware requirements are a bit above the present "norm" for personal computers. On the other hand, as buyers' expectations rise and manufacturers' prices fall, people's perceptions of an entry-level system will rapidly approach these minimum hardware requirements.

Most computers that run Windows NT will (at least initially) be PC-compatible systems. To run Windows NT, a PC-compatible computer should meet the following requirements:

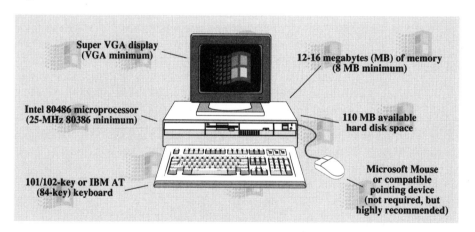

Although Windows NT runs acceptably on a computer that meets the minimum standards, most users would prefer the performance provided by a system with an 80486 (or compatible) microprocessor, a Super VGA display adapter, and at least 12 MB of memory.

Of course, one important feature of Windows NT is its ability to run on computers other than PC-compatible systems. For example, Windows NT also runs on computers that adhere to the advanced RISC computing (ARC) standard developed by a consortium of hardware and software manufacturers. This standard specifies a computer that is similar to a PC but is based on a RISC microprocessor. A RISC microprocessor is designed to use fewer internal instructions (and so is called a reduced instruction set computing, or RISC, microprocessor) so that it can execute more instructions per second. (A complex instruction set computing, or CISC, microprocessor such as the 80386 has more instructions that can perform complex operations, but because of this it can execute fewer instructions per second.) Examples of RISC microprocessors being used in ARC-compliant systems that run Windows NT are the MIPS R4000, the DEC Alpha, and the Intergraph Clipper.

ARC-compliant computers are typically used for applications requiring excellent performance on floating-point mathematical operations, such as three-dimensional modeling. Because of their added cost and their expected high performance, RISC computers typically have at least 16 MB of memory.

Particularly demanding workstation applications (such as computer-aided design, or CAD) might require more computing power than a conventional workstation can provide. Windows NT can run on certain computers built with two 80486 microprocessors to provide the additional computing power needed for such applications.

Even more powerful hardware is often required of servers on large networks. For example, a computer running a server-based database application such as Microsoft SQL Server can be expected to process hundreds of network requests every minute. These types of applications, which implement a model of computing called *client-server* computing, often replace functions previously handled by mainframe computers. To support such high-volume applications, Windows NT Advanced Server (an extended version of Windows NT) can be adapted to run on computers with up to 32 microprocessors. For such computers, Windows NT Advanced Server is specially tailored by the computer manufacturer to run on the manufacturer's particular system configuration.

The following table summarizes minimum and recommended hardware configurations for particular hardware applications:

Application	Operating system	Microprocessor(s)	Memory	Hard disk
Minimum Workstation	Windows NT	25-MHz 80386	8 MB	110 MB
Typical Workstation	Windows NT	80486	12–16 MB	200–300 MB
High-End Workstation	Windows NT	80486 (1 or 2) or RISC (1 or 2)	16+ MB	300+ MB
Minimum Server	Windows NT Advanced Server	33-MHz 80386	12 MB	100 MB
Typical Server	Windows NT Advanced Server	80486 (1 or 2) or RISC (1 or 2)	16+ MB	300+ MB (as needed)
High-Volume Server	Windows NT Advanced Server	80486 (2–32) or RISC (2–32)	32+ MB	1+ GB (as needed)

In this table, RISC microprocessors include MIPS R4000, MIPS R4400, DEC Alpha, and Intergraph Clipper microprocessors.

What kind of file systems can I use?

Windows NT can access any of a number of file systems. In addition to its own Windows NT file system (NTFS), Windows NT can also access files using the high-performance file system (HPFS) of OS/2 and the file allocation table (FAT) file system of MS-DOS. Most likely, you will want to maintain your files on an NTFS file system, a FAT file system, or a combination of the two.

A *file system* determines the way an operating system keeps track of and provides access to files on a computer's hard disk or other storage medium. Typically the file system provides a method for naming files, for organizing them (such as by listing them in a directory), for controlling how users can access them, and so on.

An operating system is usually built around a particular file system. For example, MS-DOS can directly access only files stored on a disk partition formatted for the FAT file system. Windows NT supports three different file systems:

- The FAT file system used by MS-DOS
- The HPFS file system used by OS/2
- The NTFS file system introduced with Windows NT

The following sections briefly describe these file systems:

The FAT file system

The FAT file system is the most widely used file system in the world. It was developed in 1982 to serve as the file system for MS-DOS. Because MS-DOS became the dominant operating system for personal computers, the floppy and hard disks of millions of computers have been formatted for the FAT file system. Because of this prevalence, many other operating systems also support the FAT file system as a secondary file system.

ARC-compliant computers (such as the MIPS R4000) must have at least one small FAT partition to store the information the microprocessor needs to start the system. On ARC-compliant computers running Windows NT, however, NTFS disk partitions can be used for all other storage needs, including storing the operating system files themselves.

The HPFS file system

The OS/2 high-performance file system (HPFS) was devised to address the limitations of the FAT file system that made it unsuitable for an advanced operating system. HPFS supports long filenames and provides for better error correction than does the FAT file system. Windows NT supports HPFS to make it easier to migrate from OS/2 to Windows NT.

The NTFS file system

The NTFS file system is the most advanced file system available for personal computers. Like the HPFS file system, it supports long filenames. Unlike HPFS, however, NTFS also maintains short filenames to give computers running MS-DOS or Windows 3.1 access to these files over the network. Its error-correction capabilities are more powerful than those of HPFS, allowing NTFS to correct errors "on the fly." NTFS takes advantage of the built-in security features of Windows NT to control users' access to directories and files.

If you are installing Windows NT on a PC with an existing operating system, you must decide whether to convert some or all of your hard-disk partitions (if you have more than one) to NTFS. If Windows NT is the first operating system to be installed on your PC, you should format your hard disk for NTFS. As mentioned on the previous page, ARC-compliant computers running Windows NT can use NTFS for all storage needs except for one small FAT partition necessary to store information the microprocessor needs to start the system.

If you want, you can later convert a FAT or HPFS partition to NTFS; you cannot convert an NTFS partition to any other file system, however.

Although NTFS is the preferred file system of Windows NT, in some special instances FAT is required, as mentioned above. The following table summarizes the features of the three file systems that Windows NT supports. In this table, ● indicates that the file system has the indicated feature, and ○ indicates that it does not.

File-system feature	FAT	HPFS	NTFS
Supported by Windows NT	●	●	●
Supported by OS/2	●	●	○
Supported by MS-DOS	●	○	○
File size limited only by hardware capacity	○	○	●
Features advanced fault tolerance	○	○	●
Includes built-in security features (including virus protection)	○	○	●

What are the advantages and disadvantages of the NTFS file system?

The NTFS file system provides full security access control as well as a greater degree of fault tolerance than other file systems. NTFS also supports long filenames and pathnames. When running on Windows NT, applications written for other operating systems can access files on NTFS partitions. A computer configured for both MS-DOS and Windows NT, however, cannot access NTFS disk partitions if it is running MS-DOS instead of Windows NT.

Because NTFS was developed specifically to take advantage of the advanced features of Windows NT, only NTFS provides the full benefits of Windows NT.

One of the most important of these benefits is Windows NT security. When combined with the NTFS file system, Windows NT provides the ability to specify who can access a file or directory and for what purpose. When you create a file, you can inform Windows NT which users can read the file and which users can make changes to the file. In addition, you can also specify who can list the contents of a directory and who can add files to the directory. You can prevent another user from obtaining access to a file in a directory even if the user knows the pathname of the file. This capability, known as *discretionary access control,* is available only for files on an NTFS partition.

A second significant advantage of NTFS is its advanced fault tolerance. *Fault tolerance* is the ability of a computer to correct the inevitable errors that occur when recording data on a disk. These errors occur as a result of such factors as the mechanical failure of disk drives, fluctuations in electrical voltage supplied to the computer, and defective areas on the disk. NTFS uses a technique known as *transaction logging* to keep track of the changes it makes to the hard disk. If it determines that an error occurred while data was being recorded on the hard disk, it can use the information in the transaction log to ensure that the hard disk is in a consistent state. As a result, NTFS can recover from a failure in only a few seconds instead of the minutes or hours HPFS can require, depending on the size of the HPFS partition.

Another useful feature of NTFS is its ability to give files and directories names that can contain almost any character and that are virtually unlimited in length. Instead of being confined to strict naming conventions, you can give a file whatever name makes sense to you, and you can use uppercase and lowercase letters and spaces in the name. For example, instead of naming a document file containing your March 1993 personnel report something like PERRT393.DOC, you can call it March 1993 Personnel Report.Doc. NTFS can also create short filenames to make it easy for applications designed for MS-DOS and for Windows 3.1 to use those files. (A short filename has up to eight characters in the name and up to three characters in an extension.)

Finally, NTFS is more efficient than FAT or HPFS on large disk partitions. FAT and HPFS need to set aside more space on large disk partitions than NTFS requires to store the information the file systems use to manage the files and directories on the disk partition.

The only real disadvantage of NTFS is that it is recognized only by Windows NT. When the computer is running another operating system (such as MS-DOS or OS/2), that operating system cannot access files on an NTFS partition. On the other hand, there are advantages to this limitation because other operating systems, which do not use Windows NT security controls, cannot give users uncontrolled access to files on an NTFS partition.

Even though other operating systems cannot access an NTFS partition, applications originally designed to run on other operating systems (including MS-DOS and Windows 3.1) can access NTFS files when running on Windows NT. In these cases, Windows NT provides the applications with short filenames and pathnames that conform to the requirements of the operating system for which the application was created.

What are the advantages and disadvantages of the FAT file system?

The only significant advantage of the FAT file system is that it can be accessed by computers running a variety of operating systems. A disk partition formatted for the FAT file system is essential if you plan to occasionally run MS-DOS on your computer instead of Windows NT. A FAT partition is also required as the system partition for ARC-compliant systems. Windows NT security cannot protect files on a FAT partition, however, and files on a FAT partition must have short filenames.

The FAT file system is the most widely used file system in the world. The majority of personal computers worldwide run the MS-DOS operating system, and all of those use the FAT file system exclusively. In addition, OS/2 also provides varying levels of access to disks formatted for the FAT file system.

This widespread use does not necessarily give the FAT file system an advantage over computers running Windows NT, however. The ability of different operating systems to use FAT-formatted disks is significant only if you plan to run one of those operating systems (such as MS-DOS) on your computer sometimes instead of Windows NT.

If you plan to run another operating system besides Windows NT on your computer, you must have at least one disk partition formatted for a file system that the other operating system can access. If you will also be running MS-DOS, for example, the primary partition must be formatted for the FAT file system. For more information about using multiple operating systems on your computer, see the topic "Can I keep my existing operating system?" on pages 28–29.

The primary advantage of the FAT file system, then, is that it can be accessed by any of three operating systems: MS-DOS, OS/2, or Windows NT. If your computer alternates between running MS-DOS and running Windows NT, for example, you will probably want to have at least one FAT partition on the hard disk to hold files that are to be used by both operating systems.

A disk formatted for the NTFS file system would be difficult to use on more than one computer because many of the identifiers Windows NT uses in its security system are valid only on a single computer. Because the chief purpose of floppy disks is to move files from one computer to another, Windows NT does not format floppy disks for the NTFS file system. Instead, it formats floppy disks only for the FAT file system. If you plan to use removable hard disks to share files with other computers, they must be formatted for the FAT file system.

Although a FAT disk partition can be shared by more than one operating system, its capabilities are necessarily limited to those supported by MS-DOS. Files on a FAT disk partition cannot be protected by the features of Windows NT security, even when the computer is running Windows NT. In addition, filenames on the FAT partition must be limited to eight characters, with three-character extensions.

Unless you plan to run more than one operating system on your computer, the disadvantages of the FAT file system vastly outweigh any possible advantages. If Windows NT is your computer's only operating system, your computer needs only the NTFS file system.

RISC-based computers are an exception to this rule, however. The primary partition of ARC-compliant computers must be formatted for the FAT file system. This partition need only be large enough to hold the files required to boot the computer and should not be used to store data or other application files.

Can I keep my existing operating system?

It is not necessary to limit your computer to running only one operating system. Windows NT Setup configures your computer so that you can choose from the operating systems available on your computer to run one when you start your computer. Before you set up Windows NT on a computer with an existing operating system, you should decide whether you want Windows NT to replace or supplement that operating system.

When an operating system is installed on a computer, often the operating system "takes over" the system. That is, the operating system configures the computer so that the operating system becomes the only one the computer will load from its hard disk. It does this by installing on the hard disk a program that loads the operating system automatically when the system starts or resets. This process of loading the operating system is known as *booting* the operating system because the computer seems to be starting itself as though it were pulling itself up by its own bootstraps.

On the other hand, when you install Windows NT on a computer that already has an operating system, Windows NT Setup leaves the existing operating system intact. Each time you start your computer, you can choose the operating system you want to run. This makes it easier to migrate to Windows NT gradually—it's not an "all-or-nothing" decision.

At the same time, the ability of Windows NT to run applications created for other operating systems makes it less important to be able to run those operating systems directly on your computer. Windows NT can run applications written for the following operating systems:

- Windows 3.1
- MS-DOS
- OS/2 1.x character-mode only
- POSIX-compliant operating systems

Note Some applications written for other, less secure operating systems will not run on Windows NT if those applications rely on device drivers that are not available for Windows NT or if those applications must be able to access the computer's hardware directly. The security and reliability features of Windows NT cannot allow applications to access hardware directly because that would enable the applications to bypass the operating system's security features.

With Windows NT, you do not need to have any of these other operating systems installed on your computer to run applications created for them. As a result, when you install Windows NT on your computer, you might not need to retain an existing operating system to run the applications you already have for that operating system.

Under special circumstances, you might want to be able to choose between operating systems when you boot your computer. Most likely, you will want to be able to choose between MS-DOS and Windows NT. The sections on pages 30–35 will help you decide whether that option is appropriate for you.

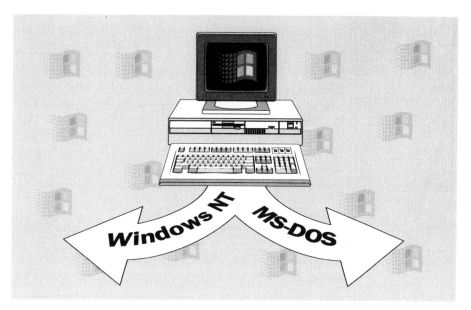

When should I set up my computer for Windows NT alone?

Because Windows NT runs nearly all MS-DOS–based and Windows 3.1–based applications, it is not necessary to have MS-DOS or Windows 3.1 installed on your computer to run their applications. You must set up your computer to run Windows NT alone if you want to use Windows NT file-system security to protect all the files on your computer's hard disk.

One of the principal objectives of Windows NT is for it to be able to run nearly every MS-DOS–based and Windows 3.1–based application just as though the application were running on its native operating system. To run these applications, Windows NT emulates MS-DOS and Windows 3.1. In effect, Windows NT "traps" the commands these applications send to their operating systems and responds as though it were MS-DOS or Windows 3.1. Windows NT presents these applications with a "virtual machine"—that is, an emulation of the hardware and software environment that these applications were designed to run on.

Because Windows NT so effectively emulates MS-DOS and Windows 3.1, you do not need to have these operating systems available on your computer except in unusual circumstances. (The section "When should I set up my computer for both Windows NT and MS-DOS?" on pages 32–33, describes these circumstances.) In fact, for a number of reasons you might want to choose *not* to run other operating systems on your computer. The following three reasons might apply:

- File-system compatibility
- File-system security
- Ease of use

The following discussion explains how these three factors can affect your decision as to whether to install Windows NT as the only operating system on your computer.

File-system compatibility

The MS-DOS and Windows 3.1 operating systems can directly access only those files residing on a disk partition formatted for the file allocation table (FAT) file system. Compared to the Windows NT file system (NTFS), however, the FAT file system is relatively primitive, lacking the advanced naming and error-recovery features of NTFS. To run MS-DOS or Windows 3.1 on your computer, you must have at least one disk partition formatted for the FAT file system, and the FAT partition(s) must contain all the files that you will need to use when running MS-DOS. Because these files are on a FAT file-system partition and not on an NTFS partition, they cannot benefit from the advanced features of NTFS.

In contrast, when running on Windows NT instead of their native operating systems, MS-DOS–based and Windows 3.1–based applications *can* access files on an NTFS disk partition. Note also that you do not need to have a FAT file-system disk partition on your computer to run these applications on Windows NT.

File-system security

One of the principal benefits of NTFS is the support it provides for the security features of Windows NT. Windows NT allows you to protect the files on an NTFS partition by controlling how users can access those files, if they are allowed to access them at all. Because running MS-DOS requires a FAT file-system partition containing all the files you will need to access while running MS-DOS, you cannot protect these files with Windows NT security. In addition, certain MS-DOS–based applications running on MS-DOS might attempt to access an NTFS partition on your computer, violating the security of files stored on that partition and possibly corrupting its data.

Ease of use

Although Windows NT is designed to support your computer's ability to run more than one operating system, this ability necessarily results in some complications not present on computers that run only one operating system.

For example, your computer might need different AUTOEXEC.BAT and CONFIG.SYS files for MS-DOS–based applications running on Windows NT and on MS-DOS itself. This requires you to maintain two versions of these files and to understand the requirements of each version.

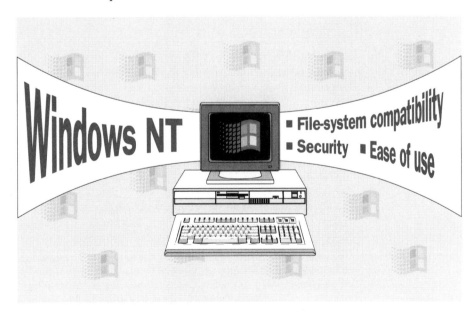

When should I set up my computer for both Windows NT and MS-DOS?

Although Windows NT can run nearly all MS-DOS–based and Windows 3.1–based applications, it cannot run those operating systems' applications that must be able to access computer hardware directly (such as ports and disk drives) instead of relying on the operating system to mediate between the two. If you must run such an application, or if you must test an application's compatibility with MS-DOS itself, your computer must be able to run both MS-DOS and Windows NT.

As noted in the previous section, Windows NT emulates MS-DOS and Windows 3.1 so that applications designed to run on these operating systems are able to run on Windows NT.

Although Windows NT presents these applications with a close approximation of a computer running MS-DOS and Windows 3.1, it must do so within the constraints imposed by its security requirements. As a result, it cannot run applications for these operating systems that bypass the operating system to gain access to certain types of hardware directly. Allowing applications direct access to hardware would give them the opportunity to bypass Windows NT security, effectively disabling its ability to protect the computer. In addition, direct access to hardware by applications makes the overall system less reliable because the operating system loses control of the hardware.

For example, certain disk utilities that recover damaged data cannot run on Windows NT because these utilities rely on their ability to control disk drives directly, without the intervention of the operating system. Windows NT cannot allow such an application to control disk drives because it could change files that the user running the application does not have permission to modify.

A second limitation of Windows NT's emulation of MS-DOS and Windows 3.1 is that it must necessarily represent only an *attempt* to copy an existing operating system. Applications that adhere to the published standards for MS-DOS and Windows 3.1 (and that don't violate Windows NT security standards) should be able to run on Windows NT. Many applications, however, use unpublished, unapproved methods for accessing MS-DOS or Windows 3.1. Wherever possible, Windows NT attempts to support these "backdoor" programming techniques, but not every one of these techniques can be anticipated.

Because the Windows NT emulation of MS-DOS and Windows 3.1 cannot reproduce unknown errors in MS-DOS and Windows 3.1, it cannot provide a suitable environment for testing the compatibility of applications with these operating systems. If you regularly write MS-DOS–based and Windows 3.1–based applications and need to ensure that they run properly with MS-DOS and Windows 3.1, you must be able to boot MS-DOS on your computer as an alternative to Windows NT.

To summarize, you should retain MS-DOS and Windows 3.1 on your computer if you need to

- Test applications to determine their compatibility with MS-DOS or Windows 3.1
- Run an MS-DOS–based or a Windows 3.1–based application that is known to be incompatible with Windows NT
- Run an MS-DOS–based or a Windows 3.1–based application that is not known to be compatible with Windows NT

In the last case, you might want to alternate between running the application using MS-DOS and Windows 3.1, and testing the application running on Windows NT. If it runs acceptably on Windows NT, you can consider converting your computer to run Windows NT only.

Of course, you can run MS-DOS and Windows 3.1 only on computers based on the Intel 80x86 family of microprocessors.

How can I convert a multiple-boot system to boot Windows NT alone?

When you no longer need to be able to boot MS-DOS, you can easily disable the multiple-boot capability temporarily by using the Control Panel System dialog box in Windows NT. To permanently convert your computer so that it will be able to boot only Windows NT, use the CONVERT utility to change the active FAT file system partition(s) on your hard drive to NTFS.

If you have chosen to retain MS-DOS on your computer, it is probably because you must be able to run an MS-DOS–based or a Windows 3.1–based application that is not compatible with Windows NT or because you must test such an application to be sure that it is actually compatible with Windows NT.

As time passes, you might determine that you no longer need to run MS-DOS (and, as a partial result, Windows 3.1) on your computer. For example, an incompatible application might be superseded by a compatible version, or an application you are testing might prove to run reliably on Windows NT.

If you decide you want to run Windows NT exclusively on your computer, you can either temporarily disable the multiple-boot feature of your computer or remove MS-DOS from your computer altogether.

Disabling the multiple-boot feature

If you cannot be sure that you will never need to run MS-DOS on your computer again, you should only disable the multiple-boot feature. If you remove MS-DOS from your computer, you can restore it only by first backing up all the files on your hard drive, reformatting the hard drive for the FAT file system, reinstalling MS-DOS on your computer, reinstalling Windows NT to enable the multiple-boot capability, and finally restoring the backed-up files.

To avoid all this, consider temporarily disabling the multiple-boot feature of your computer rather than removing MS-DOS.

The Control Panel System dialog box presents you with a dialog box with which you can choose the operating system and the length of time the multiple-boot feature is to wait for the user to select an operating system to run during a particular session. To set the multiple-boot feature to boot only Windows NT, select Windows NT as the startup operating system and set the value in the Show List For box to 0. The next time the system starts, it will immediately boot Windows NT instead of presenting the user with a choice of operating systems.

Removing MS-DOS from your computer

If you are certain you will never need to run MS-DOS on your computer again, you can remove it by following these steps:

1. Disable the multiple-boot feature of your computer as described on the previous page.

2. Delete the MS-DOS system files. The files to be deleted vary according to the version of MS-DOS installed on your computer. Consult your MS-DOS documentation for more information.

3. Run the file-system conversion utility CONVERT.EXE to convert all FAT file-system partitions to NTFS partitions.

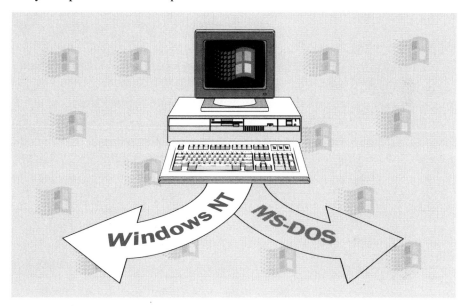

What are some alternatives to Windows NT?

Several operating systems run on the same hardware platforms as Windows NT and provide some similar features and capabilities. Among these are IBM OS/2 2.0 and UNIX. To decide which operating system is right for you, you should consider the applications available for each, the features you require (as well as the ones you don't need), and the types of hardware each operating system can run on.

Choosing a computer and an operating system can often be a "chicken-and-egg" proposition. If you choose the type of computer first (or if you already have a computer for which you are considering changing the operating system), your choice of operating system will be limited to those that can run on that particular computer platform. Conversely, if you choose an operating system first, then you can use only the type of computer that will run that operating system.

Regardless of whether you begin with the computer or with the operating system, your choice should be made after answering the following three key questions:

- What do I need the system to do for me?

    You buy a computer and an operating system so that you can meet one or more specific needs—needs that are nearly always met by the applications run by the computer and the operating system. Most people begin their search for a computer and an operating system by examining the applications that are available for each operating system and computer platform, taking into account the extent to which the applications take advantage of the operating system's features.

- How will the operating system help me do my work?

    In addition to running applications, an operating system can help (or hinder) you as you do productive work with your computer. If an operating system is difficult to learn and control, for example, you might find yourself spending too much time trying to figure out *how* to use the computer and not enough time actually *using* it. If your computer is connected to a network, the operating system should make using the network as easy as using any other part of your system.

- What computers does the operating system run on?

    Of course, if you're choosing an operating system to run on an existing computer, this question has already been answered. Even so, you should take into account whether the operating system runs only on one type of computer (such as a PC compatible) or on several kinds. You might want to choose the operating system that runs on the most types of computers to ensure that the operating system will not become obsolete along with the computer hardware it runs on.

If you are considering using Windows NT, you will want to compare it to other advanced operating systems that run on the same types of computers. The following describes the most widely used of these comparable operating systems:

IBM OS/2 2.0

OS/2 2.0 features its own graphical user interface, known as the Workplace Shell. Because of its hardware-dependent design, OS/2 2.0 runs only on 80386-based or 80486-based computers.

UNIX

First developed at AT&T's Bell Laboratories in 1969, UNIX is one of the oldest operating systems in general use. Strictly speaking, there is no single UNIX operating system. Instead, dozens of different implementations of UNIX exist, some of which are proprietary operating systems that run on a single manufacturer's hardware and others of which are able to run on PC-compatible computers. Although UNIX is generally noted for its arcane commands, some versions have been developed that feature their own graphical user interface.

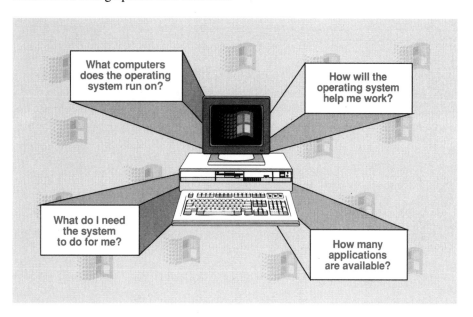

How does Windows NT compare with OS/2 2.0?

The OS/2 2.0 operating system offers its own user and programming interfaces that are not compatible with other operating systems. Windows NT features the widely used Windows user and programming interfaces. Windows NT also provides better memory protection and preemptive threaded multitasking. Windows NT is more secure, runs on more hardware platforms, has an improved file system, and provides integrated network support.

Windows NT and OS/2 2.0 both run on high-end personal computers, and both operating systems can run MS-DOS–based and Windows 3.0–based applications. As a result, comparisons are often drawn between the two operating systems. By every significant measure, however, Windows NT is the superior operating system.

OS/2 2.0 uses a proprietary graphical user interface (GUI) called the *Workplace Shell*. This interface departs significantly from the graphical user interface of earlier versions of OS/2, which was quite similar to the Windows 3.0 user interface. Users moving from Windows to OS/2 must master completely different methods for performing such common tasks as managing files and starting and working with applications. Also, Windows-based applications are not completely integrated with the Workplace Shell. For example, when changing a printer for a Windows-based application running on OS/2, a user must change the printer twice: once in the Windows-based application and once in the Workplace Shell.

A user running the same application on Windows NT does not face the same kind of problem because the Windows NT user interface is identical to Windows 3.1, the most widely used graphical user interface for personal computers. This means that users can move from low-end computers running Windows 3.1 to high-end computers running Windows NT without having to learn and cope with different user interfaces and application environments.

OS/2 2.0 has similar hardware requirements as Windows NT—but OS/2 2.0 runs *only* on computers equipped with a single 80386 or 80486 microprocessor. Unlike Windows NT, OS/2 2.0 does not support multiple microprocessors, nor can it run on RISC-based computers. The ability of Windows NT to be readily adapted to run on different types of computers ensures that an organization can run the same operating system on a broad range of computers, from desktop systems to huge multiprocessor network servers.

Practically speaking, the only advantage of OS/2 2.0 over Windows NT is its ability to run 32-bit applications specifically designed for OS/2 2.0 itself. Note, however, that OS/2 2.0 cannot run 32-bit applications developed for Windows, all of which can run on Windows NT and many of which can run on Windows 3.1. Chances are that soon more widely used applications will be adapted to be 32-bit Windows–based applications than will have been adapted for OS/2 2.0. This is because it is significantly easier to adapt an existing 16-bit Windows 3.1–based application (of which there are already thousands) to be a 32-bit Windows–based application than it is to adapt the same application for OS/2 2.0.

Despite the differences in their user interface and application availability, Windows NT and OS/2 2.0 are sometimes compared on their technical merits. Here, too, Windows NT invariably has the advantage.

For example, like Windows NT, OS/2 2.0 does not allow an application to use memory that belongs to other applications—but all interactive OS/2 applications (that is, applications that have a user interface) *do* share areas of memory with parts of the operating system. This design makes it possible for an errant application to corrupt memory on which the operating system depends, which might result in the failure of the operating system. In other words, OS/2 2.0 protects applications from each other, but it does not protect itself from those applications. In contrast, Windows NT does not allow applications to access any memory that belongs to the operating system, so no application can cause the operating system to fail.

OS/2 2.0 runs applications with preemptive multitasking and supports multiple threads within applications in a way similar to that of Windows NT. Note, however, that OS/2 2.0 uses a synchronized input model in which all user activity (such as when the user moves the mouse or presses a key) is funneled through a single queue before being dispatched to individual applications. Under this model, if an application fails to properly handle an input event and return control to the operating system, the user can no longer interact with other applications or the operating system itself. Even though the underlying operating system may continue to run, the computer appears "hung" from the user's perspective. Windows NT uses a desynchronized input model that does not wait for applications to process an input event before input events are passed to other applications.

OS/2 2.0 supports the file-allocation table (FAT) file system and high-performance file system (HPFS). Windows NT supports these file systems plus the Windows NT file system (NTFS). NTFS provides all the capabilities of HPFS, but also features almost instantaneous recovery in case of system failure, unlimited file and disk size, and automatic support for the "8.3" filenames required by MS-DOS–based and Windows 3.1–based applications.

Security is an important feature of Windows NT that is completely lacking in OS/2 2.0. OS/2 cannot prevent unauthorized people from using the computer, nor can it control the type of access granted to authorized users. Also, OS/2 2.0 does not offer the integrated networking capabilities of Windows NT. OS/2 2.0 requires additional software to work with a network, and the tools necessary to control the network are not built into OS/2's user interface as they are for Windows NT.

How does Windows NT compare with UNIX?

UNIX is less a single operating system than a standard for a group of operating systems. Dozens of different variants of UNIX exist, many of which run on only a single manufacturer's hardware. Windows NT and most forms of UNIX provide robust multitasking, although UNIX systems sometimes can be used by more than one person at the same time. There are far fewer applications (particularly popular productivity applications) available for UNIX than for Windows NT.

It is particularly difficult to compare Windows NT with UNIX because UNIX is available in so many different forms, each with its own features and shortcomings.

A brief history of the development of UNIX is essential to understanding how this situation came about. UNIX was first developed around 1969 at AT&T Corporation's Bell Laboratories. Although it was initially intended to be used only on Bell Laboratories' computers, AT&T eventually began licensing UNIX to research institutions and universities in the early 1970s. Not only did these institutions receive the executable binary files for the operating system, but they also received the source code and permission to modify it as needed. As a result, these institutions could enhance UNIX and tailor it to their particular needs.

It was at this point that UNIX ceased being a single operating system and instead became a family of operating systems as different installation sites developed their own distinct versions. One institution in particular, the University of California at Berkeley, made so many changes to the operating system that it took on characteristics of a separate family line, eventually becoming standardized in a form known as BSD (for Berkeley Software Distribution) UNIX. In the meantime, AT&T combined several variants on its own family line and announced AT&T UNIX System V, producing a second UNIX standard.

AT&T first licensed UNIX to commercial institutions in 1977. It soon became a favorite operating system for the workstations developed in the 1980s by such companies as Sun Microsystems and Hewlett-Packard. Each company tailored UNIX to run on its particular hardware. Although their versions conformed (more or less) to one of the UNIX standards, there were usually enough differences that an application written for one version could not run unmodified on other versions.

In 1979 Microsoft released its first operating system, a simplified clone of UNIX known as XENIX that ran on the first microcomputers.

In the twenty-plus years since its introduction, UNIX has been altered to work on more types of computers than any other operating system, ranging from laptop and desktop PCs to supercomputers. It has been extended to support networks (one of the earliest operating systems to do so), security, and several different graphical user interfaces.

Despite (or perhaps because of) this widespread adoption, however, UNIX remains a difficult operating system upon which to build a computing solution for most organizations. UNIX assumes different personalities when running on various types of computers. For example, the NeXT workstation's graphical user interface differs from the windowing system employed on Sun workstations, even though both are UNIX-based systems. Applications developed to run on UNIX on Digital Equipment Company workstations must be significantly revised before they can run on a PC using The Santa Cruz Operation's UNIX System V. In contrast, Windows NT–based applications need only to be recompiled (a straightforward, mechanical operation) to allow them to run on any hardware platform.

Even though UNIX's many variants make it difficult to compare with Windows NT, it is possible to find some points in common. Both are highly *portable*—that is, adaptable to a particular computer architecture. (Unlike UNIX, however, Windows NT's application programming interface remains the same on all platforms, ensuring that applications run on them all without significant modification.) When UNIX is adapted to work on a particular computer architecture, it is usually able to fully exploit that architecture's features. On a 32-bit PC-compatible computer, for example, UNIX provides applications a large amount of memory with a *flat address space* that simplifies how applications can use that memory, just as Windows NT does. See "How does Windows NT use my computer's memory?" on pages 10–11, for more information.

Windows NT and UNIX are both multitasking operating systems, and some versions of UNIX support multiple execution threads per application, just like Windows NT. Unlike Windows NT, however, many forms of UNIX support multitasking for several users, allowing terminals to be connected to a single computer so that several users can run applications on the computer at the same time. That capability was more important in the past, when computer hardware was more expensive, than it is today, when it is usually economical to give each user a desktop computer.

One area in which Windows NT has a clear advantage concerns application availability. As mentioned, UNIX systems can usually run only applications developed for their particular version of UNIX. This is especially the case if the application uses a UNIX-based graphical user interface. Some versions of UNIX are capable of running MS-DOS–based applications, and a few can even run some Windows 3.0–based applications. Most versions of UNIX can run POSIX-compliant applications. Only Windows NT, however, can run most MS-DOS–based and Windows 3.1–based applications, in addition to POSIX-compliant applications, 16-bit OS/2 1.x character-mode applications, and, of course, 32-bit applications developed specifically for Windows NT. In addition, a great number of UNIX application vendors are responding to the popularity of the Windows user interface by adapting their applications to run on Windows NT. To the extent that an operating system is useful mostly for running applications, its breadth of application support makes Windows NT a much more useful operating system than any or all versions of UNIX.

P A R T 2

Protecting Your Computer
and Its Data

What can Windows NT do to help protect my computer and its data?

Windows NT is designed to help you protect your computer hardware and the valuable data it contains. Windows NT's comprehensive security capabilities not only let you control who uses your computer and how they use it, but also help to prevent infection by computer viruses. Windows NT also gives you the ability to maintain backup copies of your computer's data with ease. And if you are using an uninterruptible power supply, Windows NT can help prevent loss of data caused by a cut in power.

At first, people used personal computers primarily as helpful tools for relatively minor support tasks, storing their data on floppy disks. The tasks were often insignificant enough that the floppy disks' damage or loss was usually not regarded as a particularly serious matter. Data critical to an organization was rarely kept on personal computers, which were often left unattended and easily accessible to almost anyone. Large organizations used secure mainframe computers to store their critical data, while small enterprises continued to use traditional pencil-and-paper records that could be easily locked up.

With the advancement of their hardware and software, however, personal computers have become a critical link in many organizations' operations, in many cases even supplanting mainframes. Personal computers are now used to receive, process, and report the information that constitutes an organization's lifeblood. Data is no longer routinely stored on floppy disks. Instead, it is kept on the computers' hard disks, where it can be retrieved rapidly and conveniently. Unfortunately, this speed and ease of retrieval also makes the data vulnerable. As a result, any operating system that is created for today's personal computers should play a central role in protecting the computer's data.

Windows NT has been designed from its core to provide for data security and protection, primarily through three facilities:

- Advanced security to control how people can access the computer's data

  Windows NT provides the highest level of security available for personal computers. Windows NT not only lets you control who can use the computer, but also the directories and files a user can manipulate when files are stored on a disk formatted for the Windows NT file system (NTFS).

- High-level support for an uninterruptible power supply

  An *uninterruptible power supply* (UPS) is a battery-backed device that provides power to the computer for a short time when the main power supply is interrupted. Coupled with human intervention, the UPS helps prevent the loss of unsaved data that might be in the computer's memory.

- An easy-to-use utility for making backup copies of the computer's data onto magnetic tape

    Regularly copying the computer's data onto magnetic tape and storing the backup copy separately makes it possible to recover that data if the computer's hard disk becomes damaged.

For more information on Windows NT security, see "How can I use Windows NT security to protect my computer and its data?" on pages 46–47. For information about controlling a UPS through Windows NT, see "How can an uninterruptible power supply protect my computer?" on pages 126–127. To learn more about using Backup, see "How can I use Backup to protect my computer's data?" on pages 128–129.

How can I use Windows NT security to protect my computer and its data?

The security features of Windows NT can help prevent data loss by ensuring that only authorized users can read or change files on an NTFS disk partition and by helping prevent infection by computer viruses. Windows NT security can also ensure that only authorized persons can change the computer's configuration or use its printer. In addition, Windows NT can record certain system-related events, at your discretion, so that you can monitor who has been using the system and for what purpose.

One of the security problems of most personal computers is that anyone who can turn on the computer and use its keyboard and monitor gains virtually unrestricted access. That person can alter the computer's configuration (even to the point of rendering it effectively unusable), read confidential files, and even delete valuable data. Even if the person does no actual harm, by using the computer without permission he or she is still trespassing.

The only way to prevent an unauthorized person from using most personal computers is to lock up the computers—in other words, to physically prevent someone from gaining access to the computers. Although often effective, this strategy detracts from two of the personal computer's intrinsic virtues: its convenience and availability.

Ironically, the computers that have provided the most restrictive controls over their use are also traditionally the ones that are the most secure physically: minicomputers and mainframe computers. Usually, these computers are kept in areas separate from their principal users, who can access them only by means of a remote terminal. But minicomputers and mainframe computers require each user to receive advance permission and prove his or her identity before using the computer.

As personal computers begin to supplant mainframe computers, many people have come to desire the same sort of security for desktop computers that protects larger computers. For this reason, Windows NT has been designed from day one to offer the security of larger computers.

Windows NT security is built into every part of the system. No one can use a computer running Windows NT unless the person has been authorized to do so and can prove that authorization.

Even when someone is permitted to use the computer, the way that person uses it can be controlled to a rather fine degree. Unless the user has been given the authority to manage the computer, the user is limited in the way he or she can change the system's configuration, and whatever changes the user makes are generally in effect only for that particular user. Users can access only those files and printers that they have permission to use, and users cannot change files for which they have permission to read only.

In addition to controlling how someone might use the computer, Windows NT can also record specific system-related events that occur during the course of that use, allowing the administrator to monitor not only what a user has done, but even what the user has attempted to do.

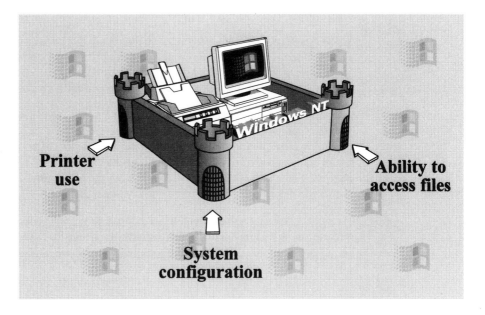

What are Windows NT's security methods?

Fundamentally, computer security is all the steps that you take to keep your system and its data safe and to prevent misuse. Windows NT provides an important component of this process by helping you control who uses the computer and how it is used.

Whether you realize it or not, you probably already practice computer security. You almost certainly keep your computer in a room or a building that can be locked when you are not present, or perhaps you lock the computer itself. You might even take further steps to protect your data from tampering, such as by transferring the data to floppy disks and hiding them in the back of a filing cabinet.

Unfortunately, the problem with these methods is that they fail to address the fundamental problem of computer security—how to protect the computer from those who are able to gain access. Although protecting the computer from intruders is important (including electronic intruders such as viruses), the computer also must be protected from authorized users who, out of malice or even simple carelessness, might misuse the computer or the data it contains.

Methods have developed over the years to provide security for multiuser computers such as mainframes. Windows NT now applies these methods to personal computers, bringing mainframe-class security to personal computers for the first time.

Windows NT uses three important security methods:

- User identification and authentication

  Windows NT allows someone to use a computer only if that person has received prior permission. A user account, created by the computer's owner, grants that permission. To access the user account, the user proves his or her identity by supplying both a user identification and a secret password. The password is shared only between the user and the computer. As long as the user keeps the password secret, no one can impersonate that user to gain access to the computer.

  A user account grants its holder a certain level of control over the computer. Administrators typically hold user accounts that grant them wide-ranging powers to manage the computer on behalf of all users, while ordinary users often hold accounts restricting them to using the computer only in ways that meet their individual needs.

- Discretionary access control

  Effective security goes beyond simply controlling a person's entry—it also controls what the user can do after gaining entry. A bank would hardly be secure if, after allowing only customers with accounts through the front door, it gave everyone inside free access to the vault. For the same reason, Windows NT controls who can modify the basic configuration of the system, ensuring that only specific users can do so. Individual users can control not only who can gain access to their files and printers but also how the files and printers can be used.

- Accountability

  True security requires that users be accountable for the actions they take. For example, a user who has permission only to change a file might unknowingly delete it. (A user who has permission to change a file also has permission to delete it because a user can effectively "delete" a file by deleting its contents. Also, a poorly constructed permissions list might give a user permission to delete a file despite the owner's intention.) By keeping a record of the action, Windows NT allows the user to be identified so he or she can explain what happened and perhaps remedy the situation. Windows NT can also create a record of persons who have attempted to gain access to a file but were prevented by Windows NT file security.

Of course, these security features alone cannot protect your computer. You still must ensure that the computer itself cannot be stolen and that users cannot start the computer with another, less secure operating system. And even more important, the security features of Windows NT can protect your computer only if you use them consistently and properly.

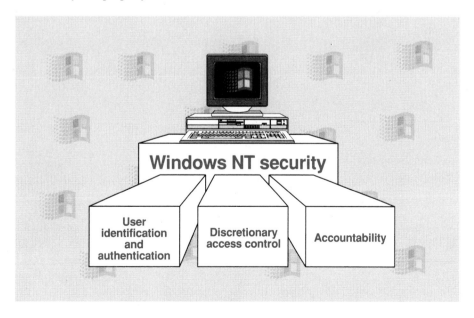

Do I really need to use Windows NT security?

You should take full advantage of the ability of Windows NT security to protect your computer if more than one person uses the computer, if you cannot prevent other people from gaining physical access to the computer, if the computer is part of a network, or if the computer is vulnerable to attack by a computer virus. Unless your computer is completely isolated, it can be misused or its data can be damaged or stolen.

Because Windows NT security is built in, you don't have to do anything special to enable it. You should follow the procedures recommended in this book, however, to take full advantage of the protection Windows NT security offers. If a hard disk is formatted for the Windows NT file system (NTFS), file-access security is automatically enabled for files and directories on that disk.

Although Windows NT can provide a high level of security if you need it, Windows NT security is designed to be as unobtrusive as possible if you choose not to take advantage of it. Note, however, that in the absence of Windows NT security or other precautionary measures of your own, your computer will be virtually as vulnerable as a PC running an operating system lacking Windows NT security.

Before deciding on the extent to which you'll use Windows NT security, consider how vulnerable your computer might be. The following paragraphs outline the principal threats to any computer:

Misuse

Personal computers are especially vulnerable to misuse. Your computer is misused anytime someone uses it for a purpose that you did not intend. Oftentimes that misuse is relatively harmless, but at other times the misuse can be problematic. For example, if someone misused your computer by installing illegally copied software on it, you might become liable for legal damages. You might consider unauthorized use of your computer akin to theft of your property—as the owner of your computer, you have the right to determine who uses it and how it is used.

Damage to data

It might seem reasonable to assume that the most common form of data destruction is damage caused by an unauthorized malicious user, a computer vandal. In fact, most data loss not caused by hardware failure is the result of carelessness or lack of understanding on the part of authorized users.

For example, a user might accidentally delete a critical system file or a file in another user's personal directory. Windows NT does not allow a user to delete a file on an NTFS disk partition, however, unless the file's owner has given the user permission.

Theft of data

One of the most overlooked security problems involves theft of data. Unlike tangible property, data can often be stolen without detection because the data is usually copied instead of being physically removed. Although offhand this might not seem as serious a problem as data destruction, the data could be used to cause harm without your knowledge.

Theft of data can be especially serious if you use your computer to store confidential information. For example, if the wrong people were to gain access to your private personnel files, you could be sued by the affected employees. You could suffer damages if a competitor were able to obtain trade secrets from your computer's files. Physicians, lawyers, accountants, and other professionals who keep confidential information about their clients could also be held legally liable if that information were obtained improperly from their computers.

Viruses and similar destructive programs

Windows NT provides an effective barrier against viruses and similar malicious programs. One way that viruses spread is by inserting themselves into operating system or program files. Because Windows NT usually allows only specially authorized users to change or replace program files, users without such authorization cannot inadvertently spread viruses to these protected files.

Some types of malicious programs (called *Trojan horse* programs) masquerade as helpful utilities or operating system commands, but instead perform destructive acts such as corrupting files or formatting disks. Because Windows NT allows a program to operate only with a user's authority, you can minimize the damage a Trojan horse program can inflict by testing it while logged on with a restricted user account. (See the section "What is a user account?" on pages 54–55 for more information on user accounts.) For example, if you log on with the Guest account to test a shareware application, Windows NT notifies you if the application attempts an action (such as formatting a disk) that is not authorized for the Guest account.

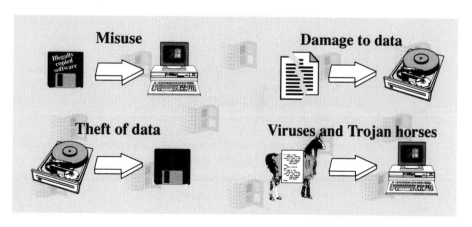

How do I let others use my computer and its resources?

An important feature of Windows NT security is the requirement that users identify themselves and then prove that they are who they claim to be. This allows Windows NT to determine whether the user is authorized to perform various functions with the computer and to permit or prevent actions as appropriate. This information is stored in the form of a user account that you create for each user.

Nothing can be truly secure if anyone has easy and unlimited access to it. A fundamental part of protecting something is controlling who can use it and what they can do with it.

Just as people put locks on doors to be sure that only those who have the key or know the combination can get in, Windows NT puts locks on your computer so that only the people you allow to use your computer can do so.

The first lock is the most important—it requires the potential user to provide his or her identity to the computer and then prove that identity by supplying a password that is known only to the identified user. This process, known as *identification and authentication*, is the essential component of computer security. For this reason, Windows NT always requires users to identify and authenticate themselves before they can run applications on the computer.

To permit someone to use the computer, you create a user account for that person. The account contains information about the user, including the user's name and the password that the user supplies to verify that he or she is the person for whom you created the account. For the sake of convenience, Windows NT provides built-in accounts that provide the basic set initially required for a single-user system.

The user requests permission to use a computer by logging on to the computer. After logging on, the user supplies a username that identifies the particular account he or she logs on to (users can have more than one account) and the password for that account. Windows NT verifies that the username and password provided match the information in the user account and then restores the user's preferences for system elements such as screen colors and mouse settings. If the user account also specifies a logon script, Windows NT runs the script. If the account specifies a home directory, Windows sets the home directory as the user's default directory. See the sections "What is a logon script?" on pages 74–75 and "What is a home directory?" on pages 76–77 for more information.

After the computer is set up according to the information stored in the user account, the user can begin running applications stored on the computer. When the user runs an application, Windows NT ensures that the user is authorized to perform everything the application attempts to do on his or her behalf. (This authorization is based on the account the user specified during the logon process.) In effect, the application runs as the user's agent, with the authority granted by the account with which the user logged on. For example, if the user account does not authorize changing the setting of the computer's internal clock, the user cannot use the Control Panel or command prompt to set the system time. If the user tries to do so, Windows NT displays an error message.

Windows NT provides for collections of user accounts known as *groups* into which a user account can be placed to give the user all the privileges and permissions associated with the group. For example, a user account belonging to the Administrators group gives the account holder full authority over the system. For more information about groups, see the sections "What is a group?" on pages 78–79 and "What are built-in groups?" on pages 80–81.

User accounts are not restricted to a single computer with which a user has direct physical access. A user with accounts on other computers that are connected to the user's own computer over a network can use those computers' resources (such as files and printers) over the network.

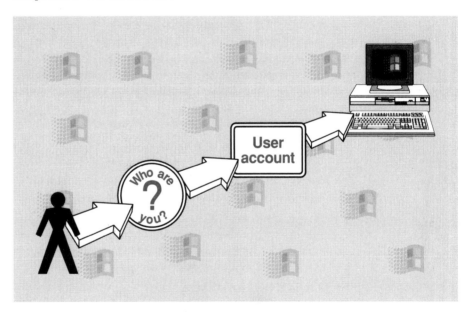

What is a user account?

A user account consists of information that Windows NT maintains about a particular user, including the user's full name, username, password, and the user's privileges for using the system. A user logs on with a particular account to gain access to the privileges and permissions associated with that account. Ordinarily, the system administrator creates accounts for individual users, but under certain circumstances other users also have the right to create user accounts.

A Windows NT user account is similar to a bank account. A bank account contains information such as the owner's name, current balance, overdraft privileges, and so on. In a similar fashion, a user account contains information about the user's identity, groups to which the user belongs, and so on. After the user has logged on with a user account, Windows NT determines whether the user is authorized to perform certain actions with the computer based on the information in the account.

Information contained in the user account includes

- The username that identifies the account. Typically, this is a shortened form of the user's full name, such as JSmith or JaneS for Jane Smith. (Using a shortened form of a person's name makes it easier to type.) Note, however, that the username can be any string of text that uniquely identifies the account. For more information, see the section "What is a username?" on pages 56–57.

- The user's full name. Although this information is optional, it might be useful if the username and the user's actual name are different.

- An optional description of the user or of the account. This might consist of the person's job title or the purpose of the account.

- The user's password. Although a password is optional, by default only the Guest account does not have a password (so that unknown users can gain network access). An account's password is normally assigned initially by the person who creates the account. The user then changes the assigned password immediately after first logging on to ensure that the password is known only by the user. For more information, see the section "What is a password?" on pages 58–59.

- Whether the account is disabled. Disabling an account prevents a user from logging on with it.

- Groups to which the user account belongs. Every user account should belong to at least one built-in group that determines the amount of control the user can exercise over the computer. For more information, see the sections "What is a group?" on pages 78–79 and "What are built-in groups?" on pages 80–81.

- Initialization information such as the user's home directory and logon script. Windows NT uses this and information saved by the user about preferred system settings to configure the computer each time the user logs on with the account. For more information, see the sections "What is a logon script?" on pages 74–75, and "What is a home directory?" on pages 76–77.

To ensure proper accountability for how an individual uses the computer and to protect the secrecy of passwords, two or more people should not share a single user account. (The exception is the Guest account, which normally has few privileges on the computer. For more information, see the section "When is the built-in Guest account used?" on pages 66–67.) Every person who uses the computer should have at least one account.

Note that an individual might have more than one account. In fact, it is common for certain individuals to have two user accounts, one for routine use and another for use when administering the computer.

As mentioned on the previous page, a user account can be associated with special privileges, usually by making the user account a member of a particular group. These privileges represent, in effect, a relaxing of normal security limits for a particular user. And even though a user might be trusted to voluntarily stay within those boundaries, the same might not be true of the applications the user runs. Any application run by the user operates with whatever privileges the user received during the logon process. As a result, an application can take action according to the user's privileges without the user's knowledge or intent.

For example, suppose that you are entrusted with managing the computer and you need to modify system files from time to time. You try out a new application, not knowing that it contains a virus which attempts to corrupt system files. If you logged on with the user account that allows you to modify system files, the virus can carry out its purpose. But if you logged on with an account that belongs to the Guests group, the virus cannot gain access and therefore is unable to corrupt the system files.

An important axiom of computer security is the *principle of least privilege*. You follow this principle by logging on with an account containing administrative privileges only when you have an immediate need to perform an action requiring those privileges. At other times, you should log on with an account granting fewer privileges to ensure that misbehaving applications cannot take advantage of an account's administrative privileges.

In Windows NT, users have privileges—applications do not. This ensures that an application can perform functions that require a special privilege only if the user has first logged on with an account that permits that privilege.

What is a username?

A username is the means by which a user identifies himself or herself to Windows NT. Often the username is a shortened version of the user's actual name, but it can be any useful text string. In addition to identifying the user, the username also specifies the account to which the user wants to gain access. Each username is associated with a particular password. The combination of username and password identifies and authenticates the user for the system.

Each user account on a Windows NT–based computer has its own unique username—no two accounts can share a username. Because each username is unique, the username provides a convenient way to identify a particular account. And because an account is nearly always (or should be) created for use by a single user, a username can often serve as the way for the user to establish his or her identity to the computer and to other users.

A username can be any string of up to 20 characters in length. Most often, a username is formed from the user's actual name—such as KimJ or KJones for a user named Kim Jones. This makes it easy for other users to identify the person for whom the user account has been created.

Sometimes it's helpful to add a prefix or postscript to the username to indicate the purpose of the account or the role the user plays on the computer while logged on with the account. For example, an account that Chris Davis uses while administering the computer could be given the username ChrisD_Admin or Admin_ChrisD.

If you use electronic mail (e-mail), database applications, or other applications that also employ usernames, it is often convenient (but not necessary) to use the same usernames for the applications and for the Windows NT user accounts.

Occasionally, for reasons of security or confidentiality, you might not want to use people's names as the basis for account usernames. In such cases, it is especially important for you to maintain records of account usernames and of the persons who have been authorized to use each account. This helps to ensure that individual users are accountable for their activities on the computer. Usernames should be easy for the assigned users to remember—or at least easy for the users to look up if they forget. As a result, employee or student identification numbers are often used as usernames.

Regardless of the method you choose, it is important to remember that a username identifies a particular user account solely for the convenience of human beings. Windows NT uses a separate method—a long series of numbers—to identify each account for internal processing. Although you can change the username of an account (a convenience if a user's real name changes, for example), you cannot change the account ID number set by Windows NT. More important, after you have created a user account and Windows NT has assigned a number to that account, the number cannot be reused.

Important Because Windows NT generates its own internal account ID number instead of identifying accounts with usernames, deleting an account permanently invalidates all controls that have been put in place on the computer for that account. For this reason, you should delete a user account only if you're certain that the user will never again need to use that account.

For example, if a user with an account whose username is PatL will not need to use the computer for awhile, you should disable the user account for PatL. *If you delete the PatL user account instead of simply disabling it, the user will not be able to use any files belonging to the original PatL account, even if you create a new user account and assign PatL as the username for the new account.*

Conversely, the internal account ID does allow the system administrator to change information such as an account's username and full name without invalidating the controls associated with the account. For example, some organizations use conventions for usernames that depend on whether a user is an employee or a contract worker. If a user's employment status were to change, you could change the username on the account without affecting the user's access to the system.

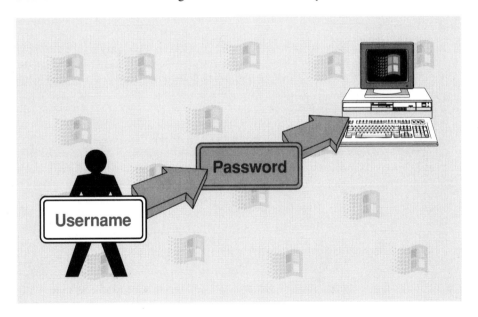

What is a password?

A password is a secret word or phrase shared between the user and the computer. The password for an account serves to verify that the user is the person authorized to use the account. No one knows the password except the user—even the system administrator cannot determine the user's password. If the user forgets the password or can no longer use the account, the system administrator has the power only to assign a new password.

A user account contains information that is public to varying degrees. Some information is often quite public, available to nearly every user. Other information is less public, so that only users with certain special privileges can view the information. The least public information in a user account is the password. The password is so secret that Windows NT never divulges a password. Rather, when someone types a password in answer to a system request, Windows NT displays asterisks (*) instead of the characters of the password.

When a password is assigned to an account, Windows NT immediately *encrypts* the password, converting its characters into a special code using a technique that provides for one-way encoding. Windows NT stores this encrypted password along with the other information about the user account and discards the original password. After the password has been set for a user account, it cannot be retrieved by any known method. In subsequent sessions, when the user logs on and types the password, Windows NT encrypts the logon password and compares it to the encrypted password stored with the user account data. If the encrypted versions match, the user is permitted to use the computer.

Because the encryption method is one way only, no one can retrieve, view, or otherwise determine the password for a user account. If a user forgets the password, another user with the proper authority (such as the system administrator) is capable only of assigning a new password for the user.

Unless the account policy allows blank passwords, every Windows NT user account must have a password. When creating a user account, the administrator usually assigns a temporary password. The system then prompts the user of the account to change the password the first time he or she logs on with the account. This provides the highest level of password security. This requirement can be disabled, however, and you can even prevent the user from being able to change the password. These options should be used only for "public" accounts such as the Guest account for which the password is not kept secret (if the guest account even has a password in the first place). Even a user who is permitted to create user accounts should not know others' passwords except as part of reenabling an account for which the user has forgotten the password. For more information, see the sections "What is a user account?" on pages 54–55 and "When is the built-in Guest account used?" on pages 66–67.

The password of an account is the key to using that account and all the privileges associated with it. Because a password can be revealed to others, or possibly even guessed, it is often the weakest link in the chain of security that protects your computer. To maintain the system's security, you must take steps to ensure that the passwords in the computer accounts remain confidential.

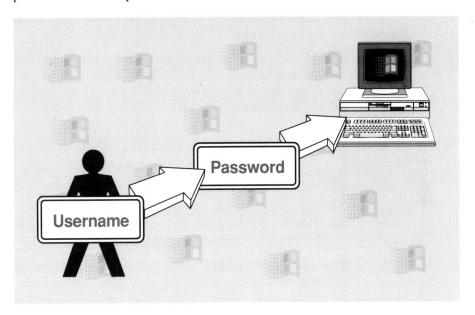

How should I protect passwords on my computer?

Because of the way Windows NT encodes passwords, a password cannot be directly exposed by the computer itself. If users are careless, however, they can inadvertently reveal their password to someone else or choose a password that is easily guessed. Protecting passwords on your computer involves educating users on how to keep their passwords secret and developing an effective password policy to help enforce that secrecy.

As noted earlier, the password of a user account is, in effect, the key that unlocks a computer. Whoever knows the password of a user account is able to log on with that account. If that person is not the authorized user, the security of the computer is breached. Password secrecy, then, is the first line of defense for computer security.

Most often a password becomes known to the wrong person when a user intentionally or inadvertently reveals the password or when a user chooses a password that is easily guessed.

Educating the people who use your computer will help them avoid allowing their passwords to fall into the wrong hands. Before you grant them access to the computer, you should be sure they understand the importance of the following principles:

- A user should never give his or her user account password to anyone, even the system administrator. The password is a secret to be shared between the user and the computer only. It is like a credit card in that it belongs to the issuing institution (in this case, the computer), not to the individual user, and so is not to be used by anyone except the authorized user.

- If the computer is not on a network, the user should enter the password only in dialog boxes that appear in response to the *secure attention sequence*—that is, after CTRL+ALT+DEL is pressed. This prevents applications posing as Windows NT from stealing the password.

- The user should never write down the password.

- The user should not employ a password that can be easily guessed by someone he or she knows. Names of family members and pets are commonly used as passwords, and for that reason the names are the first to be tried by someone trying to guess a user's password.

- The user should avoid passwords that appear in the dictionary. Some attempts to break into computers involve using standard word lists as the source of trial passwords.

- The most secure passwords are those that consist of a run-together phrase (for example, "Tobeornottobe") or an abbreviation of a phrase ("tbontb"). The phrase or abbreviation must be easy for the user to remember, but hard for someone else to guess.

You should not rely solely on your users adhering to these principles, however. Even with the best intentions, some users will become careless as the daily routine of using the computer without incident reduces their alertness. You should also establish a policy for protecting passwords that is enforced by the computer itself.

The Windows NT User Manager utility allows you to set the following requirements for passwords on your system:

Maximum age	Specifies how long a user can continue to use the same password until the system forces the user to change it.
Minimum age	Specifies how long a user must wait after changing a password until the user can change it again.
Minimum password length	Specifies how few characters a password can have.
Password uniqueness	Specifies how many different passwords the user must create before being able to reuse a password. If you set this value to more than one, you should also set a minimum age to prevent users from changing their passwords several times to return to a favorite password.

Setting an effective password policy requires you to make the policy restrictive enough to assure reasonable password protection without it becoming so burdensome that users circumvent the policy. For example, if you require users to change their passwords too often, they might become concerned about forgetting the password and write it down somewhere. Allowing users to use the same password for a long time, however, increases the chances that the password will be discovered by others. Similarly, a minimum password length that is too short allows users to select passwords that can be easily guessed simply by combining characters at random. At the same time, a minimum password length that is too long results in passwords that are difficult to remember, so users are again likely to write them down and refer to them when they log on.

The policy you establish depends on how important the computer's security is to you and to those who use the computer and on how likely it is that someone would actually try to break that security.

Even the most restrictive password policy is of little value if users leave the computer unattended while they are still logged on. For this reason, you should require your users to protect the computer with a password-protected screen saver and to lock the workstation (by using the security dialog box that is displayed when they press CTRL+ALT+DELETE) whenever they leave the computer unattended for more than a few minutes.

What are built-in accounts?

Built-in accounts are user accounts that are available on every Windows NT–based system. A Windows NT–based computer always has two built-in accounts: the built-in Administrator account and the built-in Guest account. These basic accounts are necessary to use the computer. You can also create additional accounts to give users intermediate levels of security.

When Windows NT is installed on a computer, two user accounts are automatically created, the Administrator and Guest accounts. These accounts are called *built-in* accounts because they exist on every Windows NT–based computer. You cannot delete a built-in user account, but you can disable it.

The following sections describe the two built-in accounts and provide examples of how each might be used.

The built-in Administrator account

The built-in Administrator account is the account used to manage the system's overall setup. (The Administrator account is a permanent member of the Administrators group. Groups are explained in the sections "What is a group?" on pages 78–79 and "What are built-in groups?" on pages 80–81. See also the section "Who should have an account in the Administrators built-in group?" on pages 86–87.) The person who can supply the username and password for the Administrator account has complete control of the system, including the ability to take over files owned by other users. To control the Administrator account, then, is to have total command over the system.

The Administrator account is the most important account on a Windows NT–based computer. If the Administrator account becomes unusable (for example, because the password is forgotten, or because the person who knows the password is not available), the system cannot be administered unless the computer's owner has also given another user account administrator-level privileges. Without any other such user account, the computer can be restored to a usable state only by reinstalling Windows NT.

Because of this account's importance, the computer's owner should ensure that more than one person has the ability to log on to the computer as an administrator. The person who assigns the password to the Administrator account should, if possible, create an additional user account for another person and give that account administrator-level privileges by adding the account to the Administrators group. (Depending on how you install Windows NT, Windows NT Setup might do this automatically.) As an alternative, the computer's administrator can write down the password and store it in a place accessible only to a backup administrator.

The built-in Guest account

In a sense, the built-in Guest account is the opposite of the Administrator account. By default, the Guest account has no password and belongs to the Guests group, the least-privileged group. Consequently, whoever logs on with the Guest account has limited access to the computer's resources. Note also that your computer uses the Guest account to connect a network user who lacks an account on your computer. To ensure a high degree of security, you should disable this account unless you need to provide network access to users who do not have accounts on your computer.

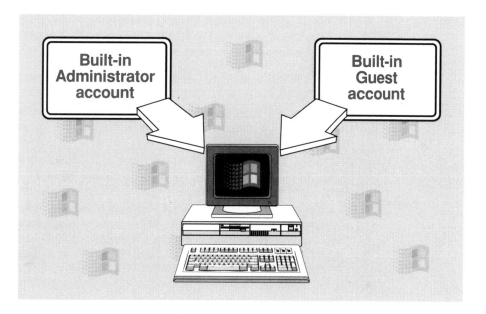

When is the built-in Administrator account used?

The built-in Administrator account has more control over the computer than any other user account. The person who logs on with the Administrator account can create, delete, and modify user accounts; share files and printers; and install and configure system software. Because of the possibility of this authority being used improperly, even without the user's intent, the holder of the Administrator account should use it only while administering the system and not for daily computer use.

The Administrator account is not only the most important user account on your computer, it is also the most powerful. The person who logs on with the Administrator account faces few limits in using the computer.

If you are not particularly concerned about keeping your system as secure as possible, you can regularly log on with the Administrator user account; this gives you the same type of control over your computer as you would have on a personal computer with no security. As an alternative, you can create a separate user account for routine use and add it to the Administrators group, thereby giving it the same privileges as the Administrator user account. (In some cases, Windows NT Setup does this automatically. See the sections "What is a group?" on pages 78–79 and "What are built-in groups?" on pages 80–81 for more information on groups.) The Administrator user account would then remain as a backup account whose password you would store in a secure place or give to someone else for use only if your everyday account became unusable.

For example, suppose Dale Porter is the primary user and administrator of a Windows NT–based computer. Dale logs on to the computer using the Administrator user account, creates an account named DaleP, and adds that account to the Administrators group. Dale then gives the password of the Administrator user account to an associate. Now Dale can log on every day as DaleP (a username Dale is also likely to use for connecting to shared resources on other computers). The associate who has the password of the Administrator user account can step in if Dale becomes unable to administer the machine (if Dale goes on vacation, perhaps) and use the Administrator user account to manage the computer.

Although this scenario illustrates the most convenient way to administer the computer on a daily basis, it does not show you how to keep the computer as secure as possible. To maintain maximum system security, you should observe the *principle of least privilege*. In other words, you should log on with the Administrator user account (or with another account that belongs to the Administrators group) only when you actually need to use the privileges associated with that account, and only for as long as necessary.

To maintain maximum security on your system, use an account belonging to the Administrators group to do only the following:

- Create, modify, or delete user accounts
- Modify or delete groups created by other users
- Add or remove users from built-in groups
- Assign special rights to a group
- Modify operating system software
- Install or upgrade application software
- Install or update device drivers
- Partition or format a hard disk
- Set up the computer for remote administration on a network

These tasks can be performed only by a user logged on with the Administrator account or with an account belonging to the Administrators group, which has all the privileges of the Administrator account.

To observe the principle of least privilege, create a separate account for using the computer every day and add it to either the Power Users or Users group. (The one you choose depends on whether the computer is on a network and on the degree of management control the user is to be given.) That way you can routinely log on with the less privileged account and not compromise system security by remaining logged on with an account that has the privileges (and potential hazards) of an account belonging to the Administrators group.

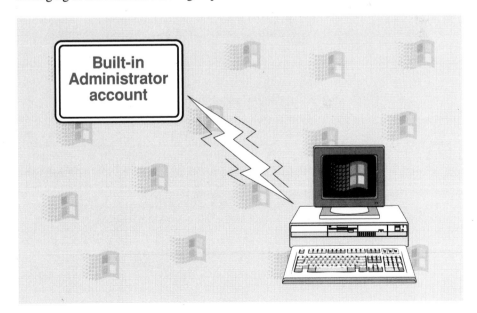

When is the built-in Guest account used?

The built-in Guest account is just the opposite of the Administrator account: The person logged on with the Guest account has limited ability to use the system. By default, Windows NT Setup creates the Guest account with no password so that anyone can log on to the computer with the Guest account.

Sometimes it is not possible or even desirable to create a separate user account for every person who will ever use a computer. For example, if you were to set up a Windows NT–based computer in an information kiosk in a public library, you could not possibly identify and create a user account for everyone who might use it.

Instead, Windows NT Setup creates a special account for unanticipated users. The built-in Guest account has the username Guest and initially no password, so that anybody who knows the username can log on with the account. You will usually want to use the Guest account to make only certain files on your system available to unanticipated users or to people whose infrequent use of the computer makes creating user accounts for each a waste of time. The Guest account enables these people to use the computer while limiting how they access the computer's resources.

You must be sure that the Guest account denies access to all directories and files except those that you explicitly want to make available to users who log on with the Guest account. One way to do this is to create a home directory for the Guest account. (See the section "What is a home directory?" on pages 76–77.) Give the Guest account Read access for the home directory, and set the permissions for all other directories to No Access (except, of course, for directories containing the operating system and the applications the guest users are to run). Your computer's users can make files available to people logged on with the Guest account by placing the files in the Guest account's home directory or its subdirectories.

Important   If your system has one or more disk partitions formatted for the FAT or HPFS file systems, you should be sure that only nonessential files are stored on them. Anyone who can log on to your computer can read, change, or delete files stored on non-NTFS disk partitions. See the section "What are the advantages and disadvantages of the FAT file system?" on pages 26–27 for more information.

To prevent people from logging on to the computer with the Guest account, use the User Manager User Rights Policy dialog box to remove the Guests and Everyone groups from the list of users granted the Local Logon right.

You can use the Guest account if your computer is connected to a network and you want all network users to be able to gain access to your computer's shared resources. The Guest account allows network users to connect to your computer's shared resources even if the users do not have a user account on your computer. If a network user attempts to connect to a shared directory or printer on your computer but does not supply the username of an account on your computer, that user is connected through the Guest account. This enables you to easily share your computer's resources with all other users on the network, if you so choose. To allow only users with accounts on your computer to gain access to a shared resource, be sure the permissions on the shared directory or printer do not allow the Guest account to gain access.

To maintain maximum security, do not grant additional rights to the Guest account, and do not add the Guest account to any built-in groups other than the built-in Guests group. For more information, see the sections "What is a group?" on pages 78–79 and "What are built-in groups?" on pages 80–81.

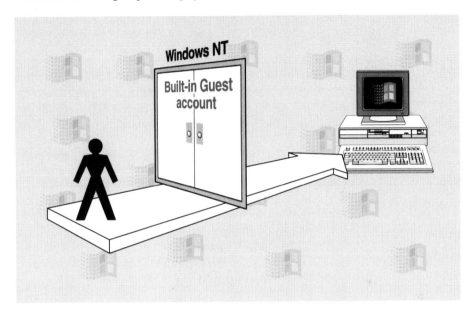

Who should have a user account?

You should create a separate user account for each person you expect to use the computer. It is especially important that anyone who can create, change, or delete files on the computer have a user account. The user account also allows each user to adapt the computer to meet specific needs.

Requiring users to log on to the computer before they can use it is an effective way to ensure that only authorized users gain access to the computer. If the only purpose of the logon process was to ensure authorized access, however, only a single password for all users would be necessary, so that anyone who knew the password would be presumed to be an authorized user.

Logging on to the computer provides another value, however. If each user logs on with his or her own account, Windows NT can do the following:

- Save and restore such user-specific preferences as program groups, screen colors, and mouse settings
- Control how the user employs files and printers, depending on the permissions placed on those resources
- Keep a record of selected actions the user carries out on the computer
- Allow the user to operate with predefined special privileges

Because people tend to have different workstyle preferences, these functions are useful only when done on behalf of individual users. They are much less effective if two or more persons share a single user account.

The following sections explain the value of these functions to you and to your computer's users.

Saving and restoring user preferences

Windows NT is designed to easily enable several users to take turns using the computer. When you create a separate account for each user, Windows NT maintains a record of each user's preferences (such as the ones the user sets in Program Manager and in the Control Panel) and restores them when the user logs on. You can also use this facility to tailor the computer's setup for each user's requirements.

Controlling how the individual uses files and printers

Effective security requires that the system prevent a user from using a file or printer unless the user has been given permission. This is possible only if each user has his or her own user account.

Keeping a record of a user's actions

Effective security calls for more than simply permitting or denying a user's action—it also requires the ability to track what the user does with a computer. Maintaining individual user accounts enables you to isolate a user's actions as recorded in Windows NT's audit logs.

Allowing the user to administer the computer

One of the purposes of computer security is to ensure that only authorized users perform actions such as adding user accounts or changing fundamental aspects of the system's configuration. To provide this protection, Windows NT lets a user perform these kinds of administrative tasks only when the user logs on with specially designated administrative accounts.

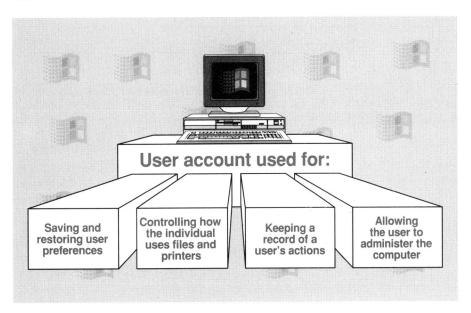

How do I create a user account?

To create a user account, you must be logged on as a member of either the Administrators group or the Power Users group. You can then use the Windows NT User Manager to create an account and assign it to the appropriate groups. You can also copy an account to use as a template with which you create other accounts with similar features.

Although creating a user account on a Windows NT–based computer is not difficult, you should not take such action lightly. The holder of a user account can use the computer and, if important data is not well protected, has the potential of damaging the data, whether intentionally or unintentionally. For this reason, you must ensure that only users who understand the responsibility involved in issuing user accounts are given the ability to create them.

When creating a new user account, you should be prepared to supply the following required information:

- The username of the account. This can consist of up to 20 characters. Although the username can contain uppercase and lowercase characters, the case of the characters is ignored when the user logs on or connects to the computer. (For example, Windows NT reads "JanS" and "jans" as the same username.) The username also cannot contain any of the following characters: " / \ [ ] : ; | = , + * ? < >

- An initial password. A password can contain up to 17 characters. Any character is legal, and case is not ignored.

You also have the option of providing the following additional information:

- The full name of the user of the account
- A description of the user or the purpose of the account
- Whether the account is disabled
- Whether the user must change the password when he or she logs on for the first time
- Whether the user can change the password
- Whether the password ever expires
- Groups to which the user account belongs
- The location of a logon script for the user
- The location of the user's home directory

Rather than entering all this information each time you create a user account, you can create one or more disabled template accounts from which you can copy to create new active accounts. Besides making it easier to create accounts, the template approach helps you maintain consistency among user accounts of a similar type.

For example, you can create template accounts for administrators and normal users. Each template would contain a username to serve as a model of the naming convention you use to distinguish among accounts created for different uses (for example, Username_Admin for administrators and Username for normal users). Each template could also contain the group or groups to which the generated user account would belong and possibly a common logon script or home directory to be shared by all user accounts of that type.

After you have created the template account (and after disabling it), you can create a user account of the appropriate type simply by copying the template account and then changing the information necessary to make the account suitable for an individual user. Note that when User Manager copies the template account, it does not copy the username, full name, password, and disabled status, as these criteria change for each new account.

After creating a new account (either by copying a template account or by making one from scratch), you can log on with the account and change user-definable preferences such as Program Manager groups to match the requirements of the particular user. The section "How do I adapt the computer to a particular user?" on pages 72–73 suggests other ways you can tailor the computer's setup to a new user.

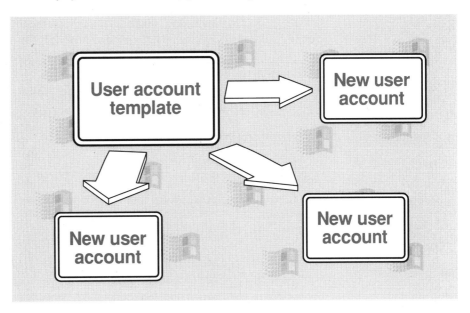

How do I adapt the computer to a particular user?

When you create an account that allows a user to log on to and interact with the computer, you can use it to tailor the computer's setup to meet the user's needs. You can configure the computer to make it easier for the person to use, and you can also impose limits on how the person can use the computer.

When you create a user account, you can specify (among other items) a logon script and a home directory to be associated with the user account. These two items (which are discussed on pages 74–77) provide a helpful way to tailor the computer's setup to each particular user. You can also control each user's computer configuration by establishing the user's initial profile.

Windows NT keeps track of changes each logged-on user makes to various preference settings and saves them in a database when the user logs off. The next time the user logs on, Windows NT restores those settings.

Windows NT saves and restores the following user preferences each time a particular user logs on:

Program Manager	All settings controlled by the Save Settings on Exit command, plus program groups and items
File Manager	All settings controlled by the Save Settings on Exit command
Command prompt	All window settings
Print Manager	Printer connections and settings
Control Panel	Color, mouse, desktop, sound, international, keyboard, and user-environment variables
Network connections	Connections to network directories, printers, and ClipBooks
Accessories and applications	All user settings for Windows NT accessories and for Windows-based applications that save preference settings for individual users
Windows NT Help	All bookmarks

With a logon script, you can set up the computer to provide each user with appropriate and separate settings for elements such as screen colors and system sounds. The logon script also makes it easy for you to remove or create Program Manager groups and to control the contents of those groups within each user account. In so doing, you can present each user with only those items he or she needs to perform routine tasks. Furthermore, to discourage users who hold accounts containing special administrative privileges from using the administrative accounts for day-to-day activities, you can remove groups and program items not pertinent to administering the computer.

To set up an initial profile for a user when you create the user account, immediately log on with the account (before the user has been told the password) and, using the utilities, accessories, and applications listed on the previous page, set up the computer the way you want it to appear to the user when he or she first logs on. When you log off, Windows NT saves the changes you made in the user's profile. Windows NT then uses this profile information to set up the user's environment when the user logs on.

Note Because the settings in the user profile are intended to be changed by the user, you cannot prevent the user from modifying the initial profile you create unless the user logs on with an account belonging to the Guests group. If you do not want the user to run certain programs (such as File Manager or the command prompt), you can use Windows NT file security to block the user's access to these programs.

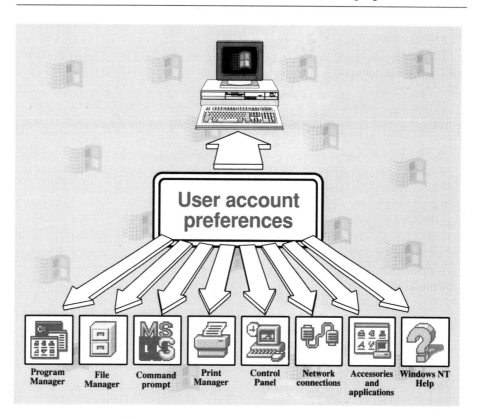

| Program Manager | File Manager | Command prompt | Print Manager | Control Panel | Network connections | Accessories and applications | Windows NT Help |

What is a logon script?

A logon script is simply a batch file or executable file that Windows NT runs on the user's workstation whenever the user logs on. Logon scripts provide a way to automatically set up each user's working environment in a way that's appropriate for that user.

Requiring users to identify themselves by logging on to the computer not only provides security, it also allows the computer to configure itself to conform to the needs and preferences of each user.

Sometimes configuring the system the same way each time a user logs on is important. For example, if a user's primary job is to enter data in a spreadsheet, you can set up the computer to run the spreadsheet automatically when the user logs on. If the user must be able to share resources provided by another computer on a network, you can set up the computer to make the required connections automatically.

These ends are achieved using a *logon script*. When a user logs on with a particular user account, Windows NT runs the logon script associated with it. The logon script can be either a batch file (a text file with the BAT or CMD extension that contains Windows NT commands) or an executable program.

Note Setting an environment variable (such as PATH) in a logon script affects only the commands and applications started by the logon script. To be available to *all* programs during a Windows session, an environment variable must be set in the AUTOEXEC.BAT file.

When you create or modify a user account, you can specify the location of the logon script for the user account. If you wish to prevent the user from changing the logon script, you can use Windows NT file security to prevent the user from doing so or even from seeing the contents of the logon script.

Windows NT also provides a Startup group in Program Manager. When a user logs on to the computer and begins a new Windows session, Windows NT runs each program item in the Startup group. With the Startup group, users can automatically start programs without having to modify the logon script.

One important difference between the logon script and the Startup group is that the logon script always executes when the user logs on to the computer. In contrast, a user can prevent the program items in the Startup group from running when he or she logs on by holding down the SHIFT key while Program Manager starts. (Note, however, that if the logon script is a batch file the user can interrupt its execution, such as by pressing CTRL+BREAK.)

The logon script provides a flexible method to tailor the system to an individual user or to a set of users. For example, suppose that a school has set up a computer in the library to be used by students of all grades to do independent research. Each student has a user account on the computer that specifies the logon script for the student's grade level. When a student logs on to the computer, Windows NT executes commands in the student's logon script that run the applications appropriate to the user's grade or a particular research project.

What is a home directory?

A home directory is a directory on the computer set aside for a specific user. Normally a user has full access to the user's own home directory and can grant other users permission to gain access to the files in that directory.

Just as it is useful to tailor a user's environment to meet his or her particular needs, so it is helpful to provide the user a particular place to store files. When you create or modify a user's account, Windows NT lets you assign a directory as the user's *home directory*. If the directory does not yet exist, User Manager creates the directory and, if the directory is on an NTFS partition, gives the user Full Control permission. When the user logs on, this home directory becomes the user's default directory.

Providing a user with a home directory serves two functions:

- A home directory enables the user and the system administrator to easily locate the user's files by keeping them in one place.

- A home directory enables the system administrator to prevent the user from accessing system files or files belonging to other users.

Locating a user's files in one place

If you've used computers for any length of time, you've probably misplaced a file more than once. In other words, you've placed the file in a directory and then subsequently forgotten the file's location. Even though you can use File Manager in Windows NT to search for the file, finding more than one file with the same name in different directories is frequently the inconvenient and sometimes risky result.

Creating and assigning a home directory for each user can help reduce such problems. Instead of searching the entire disk for a file, the user needs only to concentrate the search in his or her home directory and its subdirectories. This can be especially important for inexperienced users who might have difficulty working with complex directory hierarchies.

For example, suppose that a teacher sets up a computer in a classroom for students to use for their individual research projects. Each student is to prepare a report and store it in a file named Research Project. Because each student's file has the same name, keeping them in separate directories is essential. Creating a home directory for each student makes this requirement easier to implement.

Preventing users from accessing files located elsewhere

By itself, a home directory does not prevent a user from accessing files outside the user's home directory—it simply provides the initial default directory in which the user's applications look for and save files. (Note, however, that when User Manager creates a home directory for a particular user on an NTFS partition, initially the user alone has access to the directory.) To prevent a user from accessing files elsewhere on the system, you must ensure that the user does not have permission to access other files.

Fortunately, creating and assigning a home directory for a user makes this task easy. For example, if you want to ensure that users cannot access each other's files, you can deny each user authorization to change the permissions on his or her own home directory, thereby preventing the user from granting other users access to files in that home directory. Of course, you should set up the system this way only if it is essential to prevent users from letting others use their files.

What is a group?

A group is a name that can be used like the username of a user account but refers to a collection of user accounts. With groups, you can easily control access by a number of users to files and printers. Windows NT provides built-in groups for specifying users who have special privileges and for controlling access to system resources by different classes of users.

User accounts help control how individual users can use the computer and its resources. It is highly unlikely that these individual users will all use the computer for different purposes—never running the same applications, never working with the same files, or never using the same printers.

Groups provide a convenient way to control the access of several users who perform similar tasks on the computer. Creating a group consisting of several user accounts enables you to control the group's use of the computer. You can also control how group members use a file or printer.

For example, suppose that your computer's hard disk has a large number of directories that contain the financial information for your organization. You might not want everyone who has access to the computer to be able to view, much less change, this type of information. Without using groups, you would have to limit access to these directories and their files by specifying what a particular user would be permitted to do with the files in each directory.

Fortunately, groups can make controlling access to this information much easier. In the example noted above, you could create two groups: Financial Managers and Bookkeepers. The Financial Managers would need to view the financial information, but for reasons of control and accountability, should be prohibited from changing the information. Bookkeepers, on the other hand, who are charged with actually entering information in the financial records, would need to change the files. You would limit access by specifying that the Financial Managers group be able to read the files and that the Bookkeepers group be able to change the files. Even if each group contains only two members, you have still reduced by half the number of times you must place a control on a directory.

Although setting up protection on a directory and its files might not seem like much less work when there are few users, controlling access by group rather than by individual user account makes it easier to later grant or deny permission for using the files. If you need to give a new user access to the files, all you must do is add the user's account to the appropriate group—you needn't change the access permissions for each directory and its files.

Another benefit of using groups when protecting directories and their files is that groups make it easier to protect the directories if your computer joins a Windows NT Advanced Server domain. A Windows NT Advanced Server domain allows all user accounts to be created and maintained centrally, making them available on all workstations in the domain. (A *domain* is a set of servers and workstations that share a common set of user accounts). These user accounts can be used to log on to any computer or connect to resources on any server in the domain. If your computer becomes part of a Windows NT Advanced Server domain, you can add these domain-wide user accounts to the permissions lists of all your files simply by adding the accounts to the groups protecting those files. See Part 3 of this book for more information.

In addition to the groups you create, Windows NT provides several *built-in groups* that make it easy to give different classes of users different levels of control over the computer and to control how different classes of users access system resources. For more information about built-in groups, see the discussions on pages 80–89 and Appendix B, "Built-In Groups," on pages 189–190.

What are built-in groups?

When Windows NT is installed on a computer, special-purpose groups, called built-in groups, are created automatically. The primary purpose of most of these groups is to provide an easy way for the system administrator to divide users into groups with different levels of control over the computer. Other built-in groups do not have members, but instead refer to one or more users based on how those users are accessing the computer.

Windows NT makes it easy to govern the way various users can manage a computer. To give a user a particular level of authority over the system, the system administrator can simply add the user's account to one of five built-in groups, which include:

- Users
- Power Users
- Administrators
- Backup Operators
- Guests

Each of these groups gives the user a certain level of control over the computer, depending on the user's role. For example, to allow a user account to have the basic level of control required by someone who uses the computer regularly, you would simply add the user account to the Users group. To give the user the ability to act as a system administrator, you would add the user's account to the Administrators group. (More detailed information is provided in the sections "Who should have an account in the Users built-in group?" on pages 82–83 and "Who should have an account in the Administrators built-in group?" on pages 86–87.)

You must be logged on as a member of the Administrators group to control the membership of the Administrators or Backup Operators built-in groups. A user logged on as a member of the Power Users or Administrator group can add or remove members from the Power Users, Users, and Guests built-in groups.

Windows NT also provides other built-in groups that contain no members. Instead, these groups refer to a user based on how he or she is using the computer. Windows NT contains four such groups:

- Interactive Users

  The Interactive Users group refers to a user only if the user logs on to the computer interactively (that is, has physical access to the computer and its keyboard, mouse, and display).

- Network Users

  The Network Users group refers to any user who connects to the computer over a network (to use a printer, for example).

- Everyone

  The Everyone group refers to all users who interactively log on or use the network to connect to the computer—that is, the Interactive Users and the Network Users groups combined.

- Creator Owner

  The Creator Owner group refers to the user who has created a file, directory, or print job.

Each of these groups provides a convenient way to control access to resources by allowing you to give permission to a user based on how that person uses your computer's resources. For example, you can prevent users at other computers on a network from using certain files by denying Network Users access to the files.

The Creator Owner group provides an effective way for you to allow users who create directories, files, and print jobs appropriate access to those objects without your knowing in advance who those users will be. The permission granted the Creator Owner group acts as a "template" that determines the type of permission the user who creates the directory, file, or print job is to receive when the user creates the object.

For example, suppose you set up a directory in which you want to allow other users to create subdirectories of their own. You can give other users permission only to add and list files in the directory but give the Creator Owner group Full Control permission over the subdirectories they create. Then, when a user creates a subdirectory, the user automatically receives Full Control permission for it.

Note Permission granted to the Creator Owner for a particular "container" (such as a directory or printer) does not grant or deny access to the container itself. It controls access only to objects (such as files or print jobs) that are subsequently created in the container.

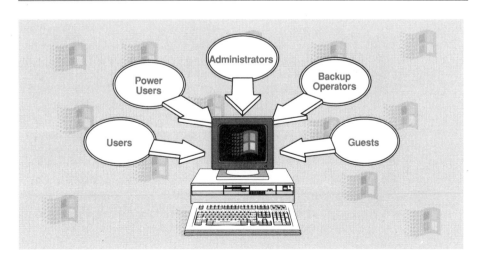

Who should have an account in the Users built-in group?

Everyone who uses a computer routinely should have an account in the Users group. Logging on with an account belonging to the Users group gives a user the necessary level of control for performing normal activities on the computer, such as running applications and managing files.

The Users built-in group provides a level of control over the computer that is necessary for routine computer use. Every user of a Windows NT–based computer should have an account that belongs to the Users group unless that user logs on solely to administer the computer. (Note, however, that if the computer is on a network, placing the user's account in the Power Users group might be more appropriate. See "Who should have an account in the Power Users built-in group?" on pages 84–85 for more information.)

Whenever User Manager creates a new user account, it automatically adds that account to the Users group. If a user has more than one account on the computer, one of those accounts should belong to the Users group and you should encourage the user to log on with that account whenever the user is not performing administrative tasks, thereby following the *principle of least privilege*. (See the discussion "What is a user account?" on pages 54–55 for more information.)

Accounts in the Administrators and Power Users groups should also be placed in the Users group. This ensures that permissions that apply to the Users groups also apply to users in the more privileged groups.

The following sections outline many of the actions a user who logs on as a member of the Users group can carry out on the computer in addition to running applications and managing files.

Creating and managing groups

Groups are crucial to using Windows NT security effectively. Users who give other users access to their files should do so by giving groups, not individual users, permission to access the files. Doing so makes it much easier to manage permissions. (See the discussion "What is a group?" on pages 78–79 for more information.)

Because of the importance of groups, all regular users of the computer must be able to create and manage their own groups. Members of the Users group can create groups and manage the groups they create, including adding user accounts, removing user accounts, and deleting groups they themselves created.

Note that when logged on as a member of the Users group, a user cannot create user accounts. Instead, the user can only add existing user accounts to his or her groups. This allows the user to control access to his or her own files, but does not permit the user to give new users access to the computer. Only a user logged on as a member of the Administrators or Power Users group can create user accounts.

Keeping a personal profile

Many aspects of a computer's configuration are mostly a matter of personal preference. For example, the choice of desktop wallpaper or the arrangement of Program Manager groups rarely affects the computer's security or integrity. It is reasonable, then, to allow users to configure their computers in a way that makes them comfortable as long as their choices don't affect the fundamental operation or security of the computers.

For this reason, Windows NT keeps track of personal preferences regarding desktop colors, mouse and keyboard settings, personal program groups, and so on. When a user logged on as a member of the Users group logs off the computer, Windows NT saves these settings and then restores them the next time that user logs on with the same account.

Connecting to a computer over a network

One of the primary purposes of a network is to give users direct access to resources (such as files and printers) on other computers. A regular user of a computer on a network should be able to connect his or her computer to other computers sharing those resources, so a user logged on as a member of the Users group has the ability to make those kinds of connections.

Who should have an account in the Power Users built-in group?

The Power Users group contains the accounts of users who are qualified to share the computer's files, printers, and ClipBook pages over the network. The Power Users group provides an appropriate level of control for effectively managing these shared resources.

Every Windows NT–based computer on a network is able to connect to and share not only resources provided by other computers, but also its own files, printers, and ClipBook pages. (ClipBook is a utility that permanently stores the contents of the Clipboard as a page in the ClipBook. Users can then copy the contents of ClipBook pages to the Clipboard so that the pages can be pasted into a document.) Without adequate controls, however, this ability to share can lead to the computer's resources being damaged, misused, or stolen.

As a result, allowing everyday users of the computer to share the computer's re-sources over the network is not always desirable. Users who log on to the computer as members of the Users group, therefore, are not allowed to make the computer's files and printers available to other computers' users over the network.

Many organizations find it necessary to limit a computer's regular users in this way. If your organization has a stringent security policy, you should be sure that only specially trained administrators implement that policy, including sharing resources over a network. The primary users of the computer log on as members of the Users group, which empowers them to connect to, but not share with other users, the computer's resources. This helps ensure that users cannot compromise the computer's security by making its resources available to others at will.

Such a division between administrative and routine users may not be useful to all organizations, however. In many organizations, security is not an overriding concern and the primary users of the organization's computers have enough training or experi-ence to manage shared resources effectively. In these organizations, allowing those primary users to share files and printers on the network at will is appropriate.

Because it would not be wise to grant all users the ability to be administrators, Windows NT provides the Power Users built-in group so that users who are not administrators can share their computers' files and printers. When a user logs on as a member of the Power Users group, that user can perform the same tasks as when logged on as a member of the Users group, plus additional tasks that allow the user to share the computer's resources. The following sections detail the most important of these tasks.

Sharing directories and ClipBook pages on the network

When a user logs on as a member of the Power Users group, the user can share a directory or ClipBook page over the network or stop sharing a directory or ClipBook page. The user can also assign permissions to the shared resource to control who can access the ClipBook page or the directory and its files, and the type of access allowed.

Installing, sharing, and managing printers

In addition to sharing directories, a user can share printers over the network when the user is logged on as a member of the Power Users group. Because sharing a printer means the user must be able to install a printer's driver software on the computer, to manage the printer's configuration, and to control how the printer is used, logging on as a member of the Power Users group lets the user perform these tasks as well.

Creating, modifying, and deleting user accounts

Sharing the computer's resources over a network is pointless if users of other computers cannot connect to those shared resources. To permit control over who can connect to the resources and how they can use the resources, such users should have a user account on the computer. (If allowed by permissions on the shared resource, network users can connect using the Guest account—but that would defeat the per-user access control provided by Windows NT.)

When a user logs on to the computer as a member of the Power Users group, the user can create user accounts to provide the computer's shared resources to network users. The user can also modify and delete the accounts that he or she has created when logged on with the Power Users account.

Adding and removing user accounts in certain built-in groups

When a new user account is created, it is automatically part of the Users built-in group (unless the account was created as a copy of an existing account, in which case it would belong to the same groups as the original account). Although this is suitable in most cases, the creator of the new user account might need to place it in a different built-in group to ensure that the user for whom the account was created can perform his or her tasks with the computer. For this reason, a user logged on as a member of the Power Users group can add or remove user accounts from the Power Users, Users, and Guests built-in groups.

Setting the computer's internal clock

Ensuring that the internal clocks of network computers are reasonably synchronized is important so that the time and date information stored for files won't vary and create confusion among users on the network. If a user is logged on as a member of the Power Users group, the user can set the computer's internal clock to synchronize the computer with others on the network.

Who should have an account in the Administrators built-in group?

Only appropriately trained users should have user accounts belonging to the Administrators group. The person who logs on as a member of the Administrators group has more control over the computer than other users do, including control over others' access to the computer and ownership of all files.

A person logged on as a member of the Administrators group has nearly unlimited power over the computer. Many of the controls provided by Windows NT security are relaxed for members of this group. Nevertheless, even when logged on as a member of the Administrators group, a user continues to be monitored by security auditing and is still restricted by file-access controls.

Because of the responsibilities and risks involved in using a user account belonging to the Administrators group, such account holders must be fully trained. It is essential that the account holder fully understand how Windows NT works, including the location and purpose of Windows NT system files and how security protects the computer. These users should also understand the ethical obligations associated with holding such an account and should be acquainted with any organizational policies that govern use of the account.

In cases where one person is the principal user of the computer, it is often appropriate for that person to have a user account in both the Administrators group and in the Users (or Power Users) group. If you are concerned about security and ensuring that the computer's primary user will not routinely use the computer while logged on with an account in the Administrators group, you should not give such an account to a regular user of the computer. Instead, you should assign another person to act as the computer's administrator.

For more information about the role of system administrators and when the use of administrative accounts is appropriate, see "When is the built-in Administrator account used?" on pages 64–65.

A person logged on as a member of the Administrators group can perform the same functions as a user logged on with a Power Users account. Note, however, that unlike members of the Power Users (and Users) groups, a user logged on as a member of the Administrators group can modify and delete user accounts and groups created by others and can assign user accounts to the Administrators and Backup Operators built-in groups.

A member of the Administrators group also has additional powers, which are described on the next page.

Managing and accessing administrative shares

An administrative share is a shared resource that is available only to users logged on with accounts belonging to the Administrators or Backup Operators groups. Such shares help these users administer or back up a Windows NT–based computer's hard disk over the network. For example, the root directory of every Windows NT–based computer on a network is automatically designated an administrative share to allow users in the Administrators and Backup Operators groups the ability to gain access to the entire hard disk over the network, regardless of the individual directories made available to other users.

Overriding a workstation lock

When a user who locked a workstation is unavailable, only a user with an account that belongs to the Administrators group can unlock it. (Note that this action logs off the user, possibly causing the user to lose work in progress.)

Formatting or partitioning a hard disk

Only a user logged on as a member of the Administrators group can use the Format command to format the computer's hard disk or use Disk Administrator to partition the computer's hard disk.

Assigning user rights

Special rights that allow users additional control over the computer can be assigned only by users logged on as members of the Administrators group. For more information about assignable rights, see "What are rights?" on pages 90–91.

Controlling audit policy

Users logged on as members of the Administrators group can control the computer's audit policy. They can also view and clear the security log.

Backing up and restoring the entire system

Backing up and restoring a computer's hard disk requires the ability to bypass NTFS file security controls, which users logged on as members of the Administrators group are able to do.

Debugging the system

Much like backing up a computer's disk files, debugging the system requires the ability to access portions of system memory that normally would be protected by Windows NT security. Users logged on as Administrators can debug the system.

Taking ownership of files and other objects

When a user is no longer available to exercise control over his or her files (or similar system objects), a user logged on as a member of the Administrators group can take ownership of the files as the first step toward allowing another user to take ownership.

Who should have an account in the Backup Operators or Guests built-in group?

The Backup Operators and Guests built-in groups are special-purpose groups intended to meet particular needs. The Backup Operators group allows its members to back up or restore files. The Guests group provides a convenient way to control access by infrequent or even anonymous users.

The Backup Operators and Guests groups are unlike the other built-in groups in that you will probably not need to add users to these groups. Nevertheless, Windows NT makes them available to simplify system administration in those uncommon cases in which they are needed.

The primary purpose of the Backup Operators group is to give its members the ability to back up and restore the system's files. Although a user who logs on as a member of the Administrators group can perform these functions, you might not always want to rely on a system administrator for such routine tasks. Adding a user account to the Backup Operator group makes it possible for that user to carry out the backup function without requiring the user to have the full level of control (and the corresponding training) of a system administrator.

Backing up files requires the ability to read the files, while restoring files from a backup tape requires the ability to write to (and thereby change) the files. Consequently, an ordinary user can back up or restore only those files for which he or she has the appropriate file permissions. As a result, bypassing those normal file-access controls to allow a single user to back up all the files on a computer is necessary.

In most cases, the Backup Operators group is used when computers are connected to a network. This allows the user with an account in the computer's Backup Operators group to connect to and back up the computer over the network. One user can have a user account in the Backup Operators groups of every computer on the network, making it possible for that one user to back up those computers over the network using a tape drive connected to only one of them.

When users of network computers share directories, those directories are usually subdirectories of the root directory of the computer's hard disk. Rarely is the root directory itself shared. Normally, being able to access only subdirectories would make it impossible to access and back up the entire contents of the hard disk over the network. Windows NT, however, automatically shares the root directory of the computer's hard disk as an *administrative share*. Users who log on as members of the Backup Operators group (as well as the Administrators group) can access all the files on a computer through these administrative shares so that they can back up the entire hard disk over the network. Other users (that is, users with accounts in the Users and Power Users groups) can connect to administrative shares but they cannot access the contents of those shares.

Adding a user account to the Backup Operators group gives that account special authority over the computer. Moving a user account to the Guests group has the opposite effect, giving the user account minimal authority.

When Windows NT is first installed on a computer, the built-in Guests group contains only one user account, the default Guest account. The primary purpose of the Guest account is to allow anyone without an account to log on to the computer or (more commonly) to connect to it over the network. If a user without an account on your computer attempts to connect to a shared resource, the user is automatically connected through the Guest account. If you want to ensure that only users with accounts on your computer can log on or connect to its shared resources, you can disable the Guest account.

If you do not disable the Guest account, you must use permissions on shared resources to control how users who connect to the resources through the Guest account can access them. For example, you might not want to allow Guest account users to change the files in a shared directory. In that case, you should be sure that the permissions for the shared directory specify that members of the Guests group can read, but not change, the directory and its files.

By giving the appropriate permissions to the Guests group rather than to the Guest account, you ensure that you will have the flexibility in the future to give the same type of permissions to specific user accounts. In other words, if DanaP has an account on your computer, but you do not want DanaP to have any more access to your computer's resources than someone logging on or connecting to your computer with the Guest account, you can move DanaP's user account from the Users group to the Guests group.

The Guests group rarely contains more than the Guest default user account itself. Note, however, that if you need to ensure that someone who logs on with a particular user account has only the same access to the computer as someone who logs on with the Guest account, you can add that particular user account to the Guests group.

What are rights?

Rights give a user the ability to bypass specific security controls. Rights also authorize a user to perform certain actions on the system. Most often, rights are assigned to a user simply by adding the user's account to a built-in group already containing the right or rights. If uncommon security requirements exist, however, the system administrator can assign certain rights directly to a group or user account.

Simply controlling who can log on to a computer is not enough to ensure that the computer remains secure—it is also necessary to control what the user can do with the computer after he or she is logged on.

One way Windows NT exercises this control is through *rights*. By assigning rights to accounts, Windows NT lets you determine which users can perform system-management functions such as backing up the computer and creating user accounts. Users who log on with accounts to which the appropriate rights have been assigned can carry out the corresponding tasks. Otherwise, Windows NT blocks users if they attempt to carry out actions for which they do not have the appropriate rights.

It is important to understand the difference between rights, which protect the system as a whole, and permissions, which protect specific objects. A permission is a rule associated with an object (usually a directory, file, or printer) that regulates the users who can have access to the object and the manner in which they can gain access to it. Most often the creator or owner of the object sets the permissions for the object.

In contrast, rights are not associated with a specific object. Instead, a right applies to the entire system—and note that a right can override permissions set on an object. For example, a user logged on as a member of the Administrators group has the right to back up the system. Doing so requires the ability to read all files on the system, including files whose owners have set permissions that explicitly deny access to all users, including members of the Administrators group. For this reason, the right to back up the system always takes precedence over all file and directory permissions.

Each of the built-in groups conveys certain rights to the user accounts that belong to it. For example, the Administrators and Backup Operators groups are automatically assigned the rights necessary to back up and restore files. The rights automatically assigned to built-in groups are usually the appropriate rights for users of accounts within those groups. For this reason, you probably will never need to assign additional rights to (or remove rights from) specific groups or user accounts.

Occasionally, however, you might need to assign a special right to a set of users. For example, by default everyone who logs on to the computer can shut down the system. It might be important, however, to prevent certain users (such as users logged on with the Guest account) from doing so. A system administrator can prevent certain users from being able to shut down the system by removing the Everybody group from the list of users assigned that right. Of course, doing so makes sense only if users cannot press the reset or power switches on the computer.

You can assign or remove rights with the User Rights Policy dialog box of User Manager if you are logged on as a member of the Administrators group. This dialog box contains a list of all the rights that can be assigned and, when a particular right is selected, the groups to which that right is assigned.

Remember, every right represents a potential loophole in the security of the computer. Because granting rights indiscriminately can effectively break down the computer's security, only members of the Administrators group can grant rights. The power to grant rights to others should be exercised with care, and only by those who understand the consequences of doing so.

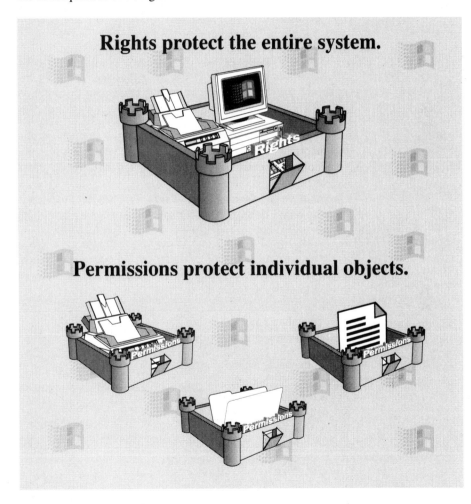

How do I revoke a user's privilege to use the computer?

Windows NT offers two methods to revoke a user's privileges. You can temporarily block someone from using your computer by disabling that user's accounts. To permanently deny a user access to your computer, you delete each account created for that user. Before deleting those user accounts, you should take ownership of all of the user's files and delete the user's profiles.

As your needs change, you might find that you no longer want someone to log on to the computer. This might happen, for example, when an employee takes a leave of absence or when a person is transferred or leaves your organization.

Before taking steps to make the person unable to log on to the computer, you must decide whether a chance exists, even if remote, that you will want the person to use the computer in the future. If so, you should only disable the individual's user accounts—not delete them. You should delete a user account only when you are certain that the account holder will *never* again need to log on with the account.

Deleting a user account is an irreversible step. Although the username of an account provides an easy way to identify the account, Windows NT considers the username to be simply another piece of information about the account. Instead of using the username, Windows NT identifies a user account by a unique numeric value that cannot be reused. *For this reason, the system administrator cannot re-create a deleted user account, even if all the information (including the username and password) in the re-created user account is the same.*

For example, if you delete an account for MartyL and then create a new account with the same username, the person who logs on with the MartyL account will not be able to use any of the files that the original MartyL had permission to use.

Unless you are certain that you will never want a specific user to log on to the computer again, you should run User Manager to merely disable the user's accounts if you want to prevent the user from being able to gain access to the computer.

After you have disabled the user accounts, a user logged on as a member of the Administrators group can use File Manager to transfer ownership of the disabled account holder's files to another user. To do this, the administrator takes ownership of the files and then gives the new owner Take Ownership permission for each file. As a final step, the new owner uses File Manager to take ownership of the files.

If you want, you can also remove the disabled user's accounts from all groups. But doing so is not necessary because the user's disabled accounts will not allow the user to log on to the computer.

Even if you are certain you'll never again want a user to log on to the computer, you should leave the user's accounts disabled for a period of time to be sure that they are the correct accounts to be removed. After the test period, a user logged on as a member of the Administrators group can delete the user's accounts from the computer by taking the following steps:

1. Use File Manager to take ownership of the user's files, if necessary.

2. Use Setup to delete the user's profiles. (See "How do I adapt the computer to a particular user?" on pages 72–73 for more information about user profiles.)

3. Use User Manager to delete the user's accounts.

Although it is most convenient to carry out these steps in the indicated order, you can follow any sequence that produces the desired results.

How do I protect my computer's files and directories?

Windows NT automatically protects files and directories stored on an NTFS disk partition. Windows NT allows a user to access a file or directory on an NTFS partition only if that user has permission. The permissions that protect a file or directory specify whether a particular user or the members of a group can access the file or directory as well as the type of access allowed. A new file inherits the permissions from the directory in which it is created. You can specify other permissions separately for each file or you can specify permissions for the directory that contains the file, in which case all files in the directory receive the directory's permissions.

Controlling who can log on to the computer is an important aspect of security, but alone it cannot do enough to protect the most valuable part of the computer—the data it stores. You probably do not want everyone who can log on or connect to the computer to be able to change or even view some of the computer's files or directories. You can control who has access to files or directories stored on NTFS disk partitions and how those files or directories can be used. This feature, known as *discretionary access control*, helps ensure that your data is used only by the people you allow to use it. For more information on the NTFS file system, see "What are the advantages and disadvantages of the NTFS file system?" on pages 24–25.

When you create a file or a directory on an NTFS disk partition, the NTFS file system records and keeps track of a range of information about the file or directory, including its names (its long name and its MS-DOS–compatible name), its size (for files only), the time it was last changed, and so on. In addition to maintaining this information, NTFS maintains a list of permissions associated with the file or directory granted to individual users and group members. This permissions list, sometimes called an *access control list* (ACL), specifies whether a user is allowed certain actions such as viewing or changing the contents of a file or listing a directory.

You can create a permissions list for each file separately, or by creating a permissions list for a directory, you can set the permissions not only for the directory but also for all the files it contains. In addition to controlling access to existing files, setting the permissions for a directory usually sets the default permissions for files that are later added to the directory.

When you apply them, directory permissions and their corresponding file permissions normally affect only the directory and its files—but not any of the directory's *existing* subdirectories and their files. Note, however, that any *new* subdirectories always automatically inherit their directory and default file permissions from the parent directory. Nevertheless, you can choose to apply the directory and file permissions to *existing* subdirectories and their files if you want to, so that existing subdirectories are protected by the same permissions as subdirectories that are created later.

Most often, the permissions that protect files are applied by setting the default file permissions for the directory in which they reside. You will rarely need to change these default permissions. For example, if you were to create a library directory in which any user could store files to be read by all other users, you would set the directory's default file permissions to grant everyone permission to read the directory's files. A user who subsequently added a file to the directory would not have to do anything to allow another user to be able to read the file—the file would automatically inherit the appropriate permission from its directory.

Directory permissions can affect whether a user has access to a file in other ways as well. In addition to providing default permissions for files, directory permissions determine whether a user can list the contents of a directory or add files to the directory.

Each permission in the permissions list for a file or directory applies to a specific user or to all the users who belong to a group. A user cannot access a file or directory unless the permissions list actually grants permission to the user, either directly by username or indirectly by a group of which the user account is a part. If the permissions list does not contain an entry for the user's account or for a group to which the user's account belongs, the user cannot use the file or directory, even if his or her user account grants a broad range of privileges.

Even if the user is logged on as a member of the Administrators group, the user cannot *use* a file or directory if the user's account does not have permission. A person logged on as a member of the Administrators group, however, always has the ability to *take ownership* of the file or directory, which ensures that files and directories remain accessible even if their owners are no longer able to use the computer.

Permissions for a file or directory are highly *granular*. In other words, each user or group has permission for a specific type of access. Some users can be given permission only to view the contents of a file or list a directory, while other users can be given permission to have full control over the file or directory, even to the point of taking ownership. Windows NT provides a convenient way to apply the most commonly used permissions, called *standard permissions*, to a file or directory, but the file's owner can also add more specific permissions called *special permissions* to more precisely control a particular user's access to a file or directory.

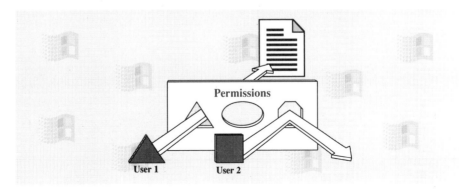

How does owning a file or directory affect my control over it?

The owner of a file or directory always has the ability to change the permissions for the file or directory, even if those permissions explicitly deny the owner access. No other user, including a user logged on as a member of the Administrators group, can change the permissions for a file or directory if that user is excluded from doing so in the permissions list. Except for a user logged on as a member of the Administrators group, no other user can take ownership of a file or directory unless first given permission to do so by its owner.

Naturally, it would not make sense to allow anyone who can log on or connect to the computer the ability to set the permissions for any file or directory. That would be like locking a door and then hanging the key on the doorknob. To maintain maximum security, the ability to set permissions for a file or directory must be restricted to a single user: the user who creates the file or directory.

Every file or directory on an NTFS partition has an owner, usually the person who created it. (Sometimes, however, ownership is initially assigned to the Administrators group instead of to an individual user when the user creates a file or directory while logged on as a member of the Administrators group.)

The No Access permission always takes precedence over other permissions. Specifying the No Access permission for a file or directory for your own user account or to any group to which your user account belongs always blocks your own ability to use the file or directory, regardless of any other permissions you might have. By the same token, giving the Everyone group No Access permission for a file or directory blocks everyone's ability to use it, even yours. In such a case, you would not be able to open the file to view or change its contents or list the files in the directory.

Note, however, that the No Access permission does not interfere with your ability to set permissions for a file or directory that you own. Even though you might not have normal access to the file or directory, you still retain the ability to remove the No Access permission for the file or directory so you can use it. In other words, you can never "lose" a file or directory that you own by blocking your own access to it—you always retain the right to set permissions for your own file or directory so you can always regain access.

When you own a file or directory, you always retain the ability to change the permissions protecting it until someone else (either someone logged on as a member of the Administrators group or another user to whom you have given permission) takes ownership of the file or directory. This ensures that no one can permanently (and probably inadvertently) block access to his or her own files or directories.

Another user can gain ownership of a file or directory in one of two ways:

- The file's owner can give another user permission to take ownership of the file or directory. The second user completes taking ownership of the file or directory by running File Manager and using the Security Owner command.

- A user logged on as a member of the Administrators group can take ownership of the file or directory and then, if desired, give another user permission to take ownership. Ownership of a file or directory can therefore be transferred even if the original owner is not available.

After a user takes ownership of a file or directory, the original owner loses control over the file or directory.

How do I give others permission to use a file or directory?

There are two ways to give a user permission to use a file or directory: directly, by adding the user to the permissions list for the file or directory, or indirectly, by adding the user to a group that is granted access to the file or directory by the permissions list. With few exceptions, you will want to use the indirect method because of the added flexibility and control it provides.

With the Permissions command in the Security menu of File Manager, you can control who uses each file or directory you own and the type of access possible. When you select a file or directory and use this command, File Manager displays the list of users and groups who have permission (or who have been denied permission) to use the file or directory, and indicates the type of permission they have been granted. To grant others permission to use the file or directory, you add the appropriate username or group name to the list and specify the type of permission to be granted.

You should use this indirect method of granting (or denying) permission to a group, even if the group contains only one or two users (including yourself), or even if you must first create the group.

By granting access permission *indirectly*, administering the permissions for a file or directory becomes easier. Most likely, you will give a particular set of users the same type of permission to use several files or directories. To assign permission *directly* to several users to use the files or directories without affecting existing permissions for those files or directories, you would have to add the permission for each user individually to each file's or directory's permissions list. As a result, to give as few as three users permission to gain access to 10 files or directories, you would be forced to edit the permissions list for *each* of the 10 files or directories. Then, to give just one additional user permission to gain access to the same files or directories, you would *again* have to edit the permissions list for *each* of the 10 files or directories.

In most cases, indirectly granting permission to use a file or directory requires fewer operations when more than one user is involved, even if you must create a group especially for the users to whom you are giving the permission. Creating a new group and adding three users to the group requires only four tasks: creating the group and then adding each of the three users to the group. Although you still must edit the permissions list for each file or directory, you need to add only the group (rather than three individual users) to the list for each file or directory. More importantly, to grant a new user permission to use the files or directories, you simply add the new user to the group.

In addition to providing streamlined administration, specifying file or directory permissions indirectly makes it easier to convert file or directory permissions if your computer becomes a member workstation of a Windows NT Advanced Server domain. Instead of having to edit each file's or directory's permissions list to include domain-wide user accounts, you simply add the domain-wide user accounts to the groups already listed in the files' or directories' permissions lists.

Because of the advantages of granting file or directory permissions indirectly, you'll rarely want to grant file or directory permissions to a user directly, even if your computer has only one principal user. You would grant permission directly only when you need to give a single user short-term access to no more than a handful of files or directories.

How can I use standard file permissions to protect a file?

Standard file permissions make it easy to prevent a user from using a file; to allow a user only to view, copy, or execute the contents of a file; to give a user permission to view and change the contents of a file; or to grant a user full control over a file.

Standard file permissions let you control not only who can use a file, but how the file can be used. Windows NT provides the following four standard file permissions to enable you to easily specify standard file permissions for a user.

No Access

Placing a user on the No Access standard file permissions list denies the user access to the file. The No Access standard file permission always overrides any other standard file permissions a user might have. For example, suppose a user has been directly given Read permission for a file but belongs to a group for which No Access has been specified. In that instance, the user cannot open the file to view its contents or perform any other action with it. Note, however, that the No Access permission does not prevent the file's owner from changing the file's permissions, an authorized user from backing up or restoring the file, or a user logged on as a member of the Administrators group from taking ownership of the file.

It is not necessary to use the No Access standard file permission to prevent a particular user from gaining access to a file because only a user who is explicitly given permission for a file can gain access. For example, suppose you want only members of the Managers group to have access to a file. In that case, you would give the appropriate standard file permission (such as Read or Change) to the Managers group and remove any existing file permissions for all other groups (or users). A user who does not have an account belonging to the Managers group will not be able to access the file.

Note, however, that the No Access standard file permission *is* useful for blocking access by a specific user who belongs to a group that has access to a file. In this case, the No Access standard file permission for the individual user prevents the specific user from gaining access to the file even though the file is available to other members of his or her group.

Because the No Access standard file permission always overrides other standard file permissions, use it with care. Use it only if you must be sure that a user or group of users cannot gain access to a file.

Read

A user with the Read standard file permission for a file can open the file to view its contents (using the appropriate application or a file browser) and can execute the file (if it is a program or batch file), but such a user is not able to save any changes to the original file.

Note, however, that with the Read standard permission for a file, the user can either copy the file or open it with an application and then make changes and save the changed version as a different file. In either case, the user is the owner of the newly created file.

The Read standard file permission also allows the user to view a file's attributes, permissions, and ownership information.

Change

When a user has the Change standard file permission for a file, the user has the same access that the Read standard file permission allows, as well as the ability to save changes to the original file. The Change standard file permission also allows the user to delete the file.

Note Some applications that were not designed to take advantage of Windows NT security save a file by saving the changed version as a new file, deleting the original file, and then renaming the new file with the name of the original file. Such actions effectively replace any file permissions associated with the original file with the default file permissions of the directory that contains the "new" file. As a result, security is usually made more effective by protecting files using a directory's default file permissions rather than by setting permissions for each individual file.

Full Control

A user who has the Full Control standard file permission for a file has complete control over the file. In addition to being able to read, execute, and change the file, such a user can change the file permissions, take ownership of the file, and even prevent the file's original owner from reestablishing ownership of the file.

Give another user the Full Control permission for a file only if you no longer need to use the file (or its contents) and you want to transfer control of the file to another user. Do not give another user Full Control if the user only needs to use the contents of the file. Instead, give the user the Read or the Change standard file permission or a special file permission as appropriate. Note, however, that you might want to give another user Full Control to allow that user to control the file in your absence.

For more information about standard file permissions see Appendix A, "Standard and Special Permissions," on pages 187–188.

How can I use special file permissions to protect a file?

Special file permissions provide a finer degree of control over the way someone else can use a file. They let the file's owner individually specify whether another user can view the contents of the file; change existing data in the file; append data to the file; execute the file; or change the attributes, permissions, or ownership of the file.

When you grant file permissions on a file-by-file basis, you will probably almost always use standard permissions. Occasionally, however, you might encounter unusual situations in which standard file permissions cannot protect certain files in the way that you need. In these cases, you will probably be able to use special file permissions to secure the files the way that you want.

Special file permissions protect files in the same way as standard file permissions. In fact, standard file permissions are simply predefined combinations of special file permissions. (The File Manager File Permissions dialog box displays one-letter abbreviations for the corresponding special file permissions next to the name of each standard file permission.) Special file permissions, however, allow you to control more precisely how a file is used.

Windows NT provides the following special file permissions, which you can use in any combination.

Read

A user with the Read special file permission for a file can open the file to view its contents but cannot save changes to the original file.

As with the Read standard file permission, the Read special file permission allows a user to copy the file or to open the file with an application, make changes, and then save the changed version as a different file. In either case, the user is the owner of the newly created file.

The Read special file permission also allows the user to view the file's attributes, permissions, and ownership information.

The Read special file permission differs from the Read standard file permission in that the Read special file permission by itself does not allow a user to execute a program or batch file.

Write

The Write special file permission allows the user to open the file to change its contents. Unless this special file permission is combined with the Read special file permission, however, the user cannot read data from the file and so must either replace the entire contents of the file or append data to the end of the file, depending on the application with which the user changes the file. Use this permission by itself only if you are certain that it is appropriate for the user to write data to the file in this way.

Unlike the Change standard file permission, the Write special file permission does not allow the user to delete the file. Note, however, that the user can open the file to replace its contents and then close the file without writing new data, resulting in an empty file and deleted data.

Execute

This special file permission allows the user to run a program file. This special file permission must be combined with the Read special file permission to allow the user to run a batch file.

Delete

The Delete special file permission allows the user to remove a file from a directory. The user must have this special file permission to be able to move or delete a file unless the user has Full Control permission for the directory containing the file.

Change Permissions

This special file permission allows the user to change a file's permissions, including any special permissions that block even the owner's access to the file. When the user has the Change Permissions special permission for a file, the user has complete control over the file.

Take Ownership

The Take Ownership special permission allows the user to become the owner of a file. If the user does take ownership, the former owner loses control over the file and can be prevented from gaining access to it.

For more information about special file permissions see Appendix A, "Standard and Special Permissions," on pages 187–188.

How can I use standard directory permissions to protect a directory?

Standard directory permissions make it easy to control whether and how a user can gain access to the contents of a directory. All standard directory permissions control access to directories, determining whether a user can list files in the directory, add or delete files in the directory, or change the directory's permissions or ownership. Most standard directory permissions also protect the files in the directory with an appropriate standard file permission.

Controlling how another user gains access to your files is an important part of keeping your system secure. Nevertheless, controlling access to specific files is only a small part of file-system security. For the greatest security, you must also be able to control the type of access another user has to your directories. Just as you can give or deny another user permission to gain access to your files, you can also give or deny another user permission to gain access to your directories. This provides an additional level of control over how a user employs your files, including even the user's ability to determine whether the files exist or not.

In addition to controlling access to the directories themselves, standard directory permissions often provide standard file permissions that protect files in a directory. That is, many standard directory permissions include default standard file permissions that control access to a directory's existing files as well as to files that are later added to the directory. (Subdirectories added to a directory always inherit the standard directory permissions and default standard file permissions of the parent directory.) When you set the standard permissions for a directory, you can also apply those permissions to its subdirectories and their files. This ensures that all the contents of a directory, including all its files and subdirectories (and the subdirectories' files) are uniformly protected.

Windows NT provides the following seven standard directory permissions to make it easier to specify permissions regarding how another user can gain access to your directories and to their files.

No Access

When you specify the No Access standard directory permission, a user cannot list files included in the directory. In addition, all files in the directory are marked with the No Access standard file permission, so another user cannot gain access to the files even if he or she already knows the names of the files included in the directory.

List

The List standard directory permission allows a user to list files included in the directory (for example, using File Manager or the **dir** command at the Windows NT command prompt) and to gain access to its subdirectories. A user with only the List permission cannot view or create files in the directory. If another user who has permission to add files adds them to the directory, a user with only List permission is not automatically given permission to use those files. The List directory permission does not specify a standard permission for either new or existing files in the directory.

Read

The Read standard directory permission allows a user to list and view files and subdirectories in the directory. The user cannot create files in the directory. The user automatically receives the Read standard file permission for files in the directory.

Add

Although the Add standard directory permission allows a user to create files in the directory, it does not allow the user to list files included in the directory. A user does not automatically receive standard directory permission to gain access to files in the directory (including files that the user has created) because the Add standard directory permission also does not specify a permission for new or existing files in the directory.

Add & Read

If a user is given the Add & Read standard directory permission, he or she has the same access as permitted by the Read directory permission, plus the user can create files in the directory. A user with the Add & Read standard directory permission automatically receives the Read standard file permission for files included in the directory.

Change

The Change standard directory permission allows a user to create, view, and list files and subdirectories in the directory. With the Change standard directory permission a user can also display and change the directory's attributes. A user with the Change standard directory permission automatically receives the Change standard file permission for files included in the directory.

Full Control

When a user has the Full Control standard directory permission, the user can create, view, and list files in the directory; display and change the directory's attributes and permissions; and take ownership of the directory. A user with the Full Control standard directory permission automatically receives the Full Control standard file permission for files included in the directory. Note, however, that even if a user with the Full Control standard directory permission is later given only Read permission for a file included in the directory, the user can still delete that file.

For more information about standard directory permissions see Appendix A, "Standard and Special Permissions," on pages 187–188.

How can I use special directory permissions to protect a directory?

Special directory permissions provide you with more precise control over the way someone can use a directory. They let you specify whether a user can list files in the directory, add files to the directory, delete files from the directory, traverse the directory to gain access to a subdirectory, or change the permissions or ownership of the directory.

You will probably find that you can use standard directory permissions to control access to most of your directories and their files. Occasionally, however, you might find that you need to control access to a directory in a way not provided by the standard directory permissions. In such cases, you can probably use special directory permissions to secure the directories in the way you want.

Special directory permissions protect directories in the same way as standard directory permissions. In fact, standard directory permissions are simply predefined combinations of special directory permissions and special file permissions.

Unlike standard directory permissions, however, special directory permissions do not specify the default file permissions for files in the directory. Instead, the default file permissions are retained from the previous setting for the user or group. If you use a special directory permission to control access to a directory, you should be certain that the corresponding default file permission is appropriate.

Windows NT provides the following special directory permissions, which you can use in any combination:

Read
With the Read special directory permission, the user can view the names of files included in the directory, as well as the attributes of the directory itself.

Write
The Write special directory permission allows the user to create new files in the directory and to change the attributes of the directory itself.

Note Some applications that were not designed to take advantage of Windows NT security save files by saving the changed version as a new file, deleting the original file, and then renaming the new file with the name of the original file. Unless a user has permission to create new files in a directory, he or she cannot change existing files with these applications.

Execute

A user who has the Execute special directory permission can "traverse" the directory to gain access to its subdirectories. Lacking the Execute special directory permission prevents a user from using files in any of the directory's subdirectories, regardless of the special permissions associated with those subdirectories or their files.

Normally, however, this special directory permission has no practical effect because all users (that is, members of the Everyone group) have the Bypass Traverse Checking right by default. The Bypass Traverse Checking right allows the user to traverse a directory even if the user does not have the Execute special directory permission for the directory. To prevent users from traversing directories for which they do not have the Execute special directory permission, use the User Rights Policy dialog box to remove the Everyone group from the list of users granted the Bypass Traverse Checking right.

The Execute special directory permission also allows the user to view the directory's permissions and ownership information.

Delete

A user with the Delete special directory permission can delete the directory if it is empty. If the directory is not empty, the user must also have the Read and Write special directory permissions (or a standard permission that includes those special permissions) and the Delete permission for its files to delete the directory.

Change Permissions

The Change Permissions special directory permission permits the user to change the directory permissions that control access to the directory, including any special directory permissions that would block the owner's access to the directory. If the user has the Change Permissions special directory permission for a directory, the user has control over the directory and can even change the directory's permissions to gain ownership of the directory. Note, however, that the Change Permissions special directory permission does not affect the user's ability to gain access to or change the permissions of files or subdirectories contained within the directory.

Take Ownership

The Take Ownership special directory permission allows the user to become the owner of a directory. If the user does take ownership, the former owner loses control of the directory and can be prevented from having further access to the directory. The Take Ownership special directory permission does not affect the owner's access to or ownership of files or subdirectories contained within the directory, however.

For more information about special directory permissions see Appendix A, "Standard and Special Permissions," on pages 187–188.

What's the difference between "No Access" and "Access Not Specified"?

Giving a user or a group the No Access permission blocks that user or all members of the group from using a file or directory until the No Access permission is removed. The Access Not Specified option permits you to specify a permission for a directory without specifying a default permission for files included in the directory. This blocks a user or members of a group only if permission to gain access to the files is not provided in some other way.

When you use a standard directory permission to grant a user or a group access to a directory, each file in that directory is protected by a corresponding file permission for the user or group. For example, if you give the Read standard directory permission to the Managers group, members of that group also have the Read standard file permission for any files included in the directory.

If you assign a special directory permission for a user or a group, however, you can choose not to automatically give the user or group permission to use files in that directory. You do this by selecting the Access Not Specified option in the Special New File Access dialog box of File Manager when setting permissions for the user or group. This removes any permission for the user or group from the permissions list of each file in the directory, and the user or group is not given permission to access files added later to the directory. Note that this might or might not prevent the user or group members from using a file, depending on other permissions that protect the file.

Important   If a directory has no default file permissions, all users (that is, members of the Everyone group) automatically receive Full Control permission for any file added to the directory.

Suppose, for example, that you create a directory named Public and give the Everyone group the Add standard directory permission (which does not specify a default file permission for the directory). Anyone who logs on to the computer can add files to the directory, but he or she does not automatically have permission to gain access to those files. If, however, the directory's permissions list contains an entry granting the Managers group the Read standard directory permission, any user who logs on as a member of the Managers group can view the contents of new files in the directory.

Using the Access Not Specified option for files does not provide the same protection as specifying the No Access permission for the user or group, however. The No Access permission always blocks access to a file or directory, even if other permissions would otherwise allow it. If, in the preceding example, the No Access special file permission were assigned to the Managers group and the Read file permission were assigned to the Everyone group, all members of the Everyone group would be able to view the contents of the files *except* members of the Managers group.

The following table shows the effects of specifying No Access and Access Not Specified for existing files in a directory. For each combination of groups and types of access, ● indicates that members of the group can use a protected file, while ○ indicates that members of the group cannot use a protected file (with noted exceptions). All members of the Managers group belong to the Everyone group. No other permissions protect the files.

Combination	Managers	Everyone
Managers: No Access Everyone: Read	○	● (except members of Managers group)
Managers: Access Not Specified Everyone: Read	●	●
Managers: Read Everyone: Access Not Specified	●	○ (except members of Managers group)
Managers: Read Everyone: No Access	○	○
Managers: Access Not Specified Everyone: Access Not Specified	○	○
Managers: No Access Everyone: No Access	○	○

For more information see Appendix A, "Standard and Special Permissions," on pages 187–188.

What happens when I copy or move a file or directory?

When you copy or move a file or directory, you must have the appropriate permissions for the source file or directory as well as for the directory to which the file or directory is being copied or moved. The permissions that protect the file or directory after it has been copied or moved depend on the type of operation that was performed.

To understand how files and directories are protected by permissions, it is important to recognize that files and directories are merely *containers* that hold objects. Directories are containers that hold files and other directories (that is, their subdirectories). Files are containers that hold programs or data. Attributes, permissions, and ownership are properties of the container, not of the objects within those containers. To avoid confusion during this discussion, the term "subdirectory" is not used below and on the next page. Instead, the term "directory" is used throughout except in those instances where drawing a distinction between "parent directory" and "child directory" becomes necessary. Furthermore, the word "container" is often used as a generic term to refer to either directories or files (or both).

Important If a directory has no default file permissions, all users (that is, members of the Everyone group) automatically receive Full Control permission for any file added to the directory.

Copying a file or directory

To copy a file or directory container, Windows NT creates a new container and then copies the objects in the original container to the new container.

To be able to copy a container and its contents, the user must have the Read special permission (or at least the Read standard permission) for the source container and the Write special permission (or a standard permission that includes the Write special permission) for the target directory where the new container is to reside. The container being copied inherits its permissions from the target directory to which it is being copied: If the container being copied is a file, then the file inherits the default file permissions of its target directory; if the container being copied is a directory, then the directory inherits the directory permissions of its target parent directory. Any files contained in the copied directory (now a child directory of the target parent directory) inherit the child directory's default file permissions (which in turn were inherited from the child directory's parent directory).

In the case of a file that is copied to a new file in the same directory, the new file receives the default file permissions of the directory. Because of this, it might appear that the permissions that protect a file change to the directory's default file permissions whenever the file is changed. This might occur when an application that was not created to work with Windows NT file security saves changes to a file. Many of these applications save changes to an existing file by creating a new file, saving the changed data in the new file, deleting the original file, and then giving the new file the same name as the original file. Because a new file is created to receive the changed data, the new file inherits the directory's permissions instead of retaining the permissions of the original file.

Moving a file or directory

Unlike the copy command, the move operation draws a distinction between whether the move operation is taking place between different disks or whether the move operation is taking place within the same disk.

Note that if a user has Full Control permission for a directory, the user can move a child directory or file in that directory as long as the user does not have the No Access permission for the child directory or file.

Moving a file or directory between different disks

When moving a container from one disk to another, the move operation is similar to the copy operation: Windows NT creates a new container, copies the objects in the original container to the new container, but then deletes the original container. To be able to move a file or directory container and its contents between different disks, the user must have the Read and Delete special permissions for the source container (or a standard permission that includes these special permissions) and the Write special permission (or a corresponding standard permission) for the target directory in which the new container is to reside. The container being moved inherits its permissions from the target directory on the disk to which it is being moved: If the container being moved is a file, then the file inherits the default file permissions of its target directory on the new disk; if the container being moved is a directory, then the directory inherits the directory permissions of its target parent directory on the new disk. Any files contained in the moved directory (now a child directory of the target parent directory) on the new disk inherit the child directory's default file permissions (which in turn were inherited from the child directory's parent directory on the new disk).

Moving a file or directory on the same disk

Windows NT doesn't create a new container when moving a file or directory to a different place on the same disk; instead, Windows NT merely changes the pathname of the container being moved to indicate its new "location" on the disk. As a result, during a move operation that happens on a single disk, the permissions of the moved container are not changed. To move a file container or directory container and its contents on the same disk, the user must have the same permissions for the source and target containers as when moving the container to another disk.

How do user and group permissions work together?

If you assign permissions to a user and to one or more groups to which the user belongs, the permissions combine so that the user has all the permissions granted to the user and to the user's groups. An exception is the No Access permission, which always overrides any permissions given a user or a group to which the user belongs.

Groups provide a convenient way of giving more than one user permission to use a file. For example, if you are working on a project for which you and several others need access to the same file, you can create a group and place the user accounts of the project team members in the group. You can then give the group permission to use the file instead of having to give each team member the same permission individually.

Sometimes you do not want all the members of a group to have the same type of access. In the preceding example, suppose there were three other project team members and two of them needed only to view the contents of the file, while the third member needed to change the file's contents. To apply the appropriate permissions to the file, you must understand how the NTFS file system combines permissions given to a user. (For more information on the NTFS file system, see the section "What are the advantages and disadvantages of the NTFS file system?" on pages 24–25.)

A user can be given permission to use a file in more than one entry in the file's permissions list. For instance, the user can be given one type of permission directly, while another type of permission is granted to a group to which the user belongs. When this happens, the user receives all the permissions granted by the combined entries.

In the project example, then, you would give the project group permission to view the contents of the file and give the third project member individual permission to change the file.

The only exception to the way in which permissions accumulate involves the No Access permission. The No Access permission specifies that a user cannot have access to a file for any purpose, regardless of whether the user is given permission to use the file through other means. In other words, if the user or any group to which the user belongs is given the No Access permission for a file, the user cannot gain access to the file, even if other entries in the permissions list would otherwise permit access.

For instance, suppose JeanB belongs to the Testers group and to the Reviewers group. A certain file's permissions list gives JeanB permission to change the file and gives the Testers group permission to view the contents of the file, but the permissions list specifies the No Access permission for the Reviewers group. Even though JeanB is directly given permission to change the file, JeanB cannot because a group to which JeanB belongs has the No Access permission for the file.

The following table illustrates how permissions for a user and groups interact. No Access, Read, and Change are standard permissions. Take Ownership is a special permission. For the purposes of this example, KimR belongs to the Managers and Officers groups. Each row in the table represents some possible combination of permissions for KimR and the two groups to which she belongs in a permissions list. If a table entry is blank, no entry exists in the list for the user or group.

KimR's permission	Managers' permission	Officers' permission	KimR's effective permission
Read	Read		Read
Change		Read	Change
	Change	Read	Change
Take Ownership	Read	Change	Take Ownership, Change
No Access	Read	Change	No Access
Change	No Access		No Access

How do I control who is able to use my computer's printer?

Controlling who is able to use your printer and how they use it is much like controlling access to a file or a directory. When you set up or configure a printer using Print Manager, you can use standard permissions to specify whether a given user can use or administer the printer.

Windows NT uses essentially the same method for controlling access to devices such as printers as it does to control access to file resources. That is, a particular user can gain access to a printer only if the user has permission to use it. A printer can have an owner, and that owner has the same level of control over the printer as the owner of a file or directory has.

By default, all users of a computer have the right to use its printer(s), either when logged on interactively (in other words, when using the computer's keyboard at that moment) or, if the printer is shared on the network, when connected to the computer over the network. The printers' owner, however, can use permissions to allow network users to use certain printers or can use permissions to control network access to some or all printers. For instance, the printers' owner can use permissions to allow specific groups of users access to particular printers, while preventing all other users from using them.

Suppose your computer has a printer that is loaded with check blanks, and you do not want anyone who can connect to your computer to automatically be able to use that printer. By setting the appropriate permissions, you can enforce a policy that allows only specific users to use the printer.

As with permissions for files and directories, permissions for access to a printer that are granted to a user and to the user's groups combine. That is, if you assign permissions to a user and to one or more groups to which the user belongs, the permissions coalesce so that the user has all the permissions granted to the user and to the groups. An exception is the No Access permission, which always overrides any other permissions given to a user or to a group to which the user belongs.

Windows NT provides the following standard permissions to control access to printers. There are no special permissions.

No Access

The No Access permission prevents a user from using the printer for any purpose. The user cannot send documents to the printer, nor can the user list or control documents waiting to be printed.

Print

This permission allows the user to send documents to the printer and to list documents waiting to be printed. The user can set up the printer for his or her own documents only.

Administer Documents

A user with the Administer Documents permission can pause and resume printing and delete documents from the print queue. Sometimes this permission is assigned to a built-in or user-defined group to allow a user logged on as a member of the group to administer documents on behalf of other users. Most often, however, this permission is given only to the Creator Owner built-in group, which allows each user who sends a document to the printer to administer the document.

Administer

The Administer permission allows the user to send documents to the printer, list documents in the print queue, pause and resume the printer, delete documents owned by any user in the print queue, configure all aspects of the printer, share the printer on the network, and remove the printer from the computer.

How can I track how others are using my computer?

In addition to controlling who can use your computer and how it can be used, you must be able to monitor each person's use of the computer so you can detect any misuse. Windows NT can help you by auditing many of the actions that a user takes with your computer.

The security features of Windows NT make it easy for you to protect your computer and its data. When you take advantage of these features as part of a well-planned security policy, you can specify who can use your computer, the extent to which others can manage the computer, and whether and how others can use various files and printers.

These features alone cannot keep your computer totally secure, however. No matter how carefully security is implemented, gaps inevitably result that a malicious user can locate and exploit. And even if the scenario of a user intentionally trying to breach your computer's security is unlikely, a well-meaning user can accidentally stumble through a gap and inadvertently destroy important data or otherwise compromise your computer's security.

For these reasons, it is not enough simply to control who uses the computer and the resources to which each user has access—you must also be able to monitor each user.

The following considerations suggest some aspects of others' use of the computer that you should be able to monitor:

- You should know who logs on to the computer and when. For instance, if a user routinely logs on as a member of the Administrators group, you might either want to discuss with the user the importance of logging on with fewer privileges or restrict the user's privileges. (For more information, see the discussion of the principle of least privilege in the section "What is a user account?" on pages 54–55.) Also, a particular user logging on to the computer at unusual times might indicate that an unauthorized person is logging on with the user's account.

- You should know when a user attempts to perform actions that require special privileges or that affect the security setup of the computer. With this information, you can determine whether a user who logs on with an account that has special privileges is using those privileges appropriately and, if not, how to train the user to use them properly.

- You should know who gains access to sensitive files and when. This can allow you to detect whether a user is browsing in areas that might not be appropriate for that user. Sometimes curiosity leads a user to try to gain access to files containing confidential data or data that belongs to others.

- You should know who deletes or changes certain important files. For example, if you determine that someone has put incorrect information in a file, you can find out who changed the file and, with that user's help, correct the file's contents. This can also help you detect when a virus is attempting to infect system or program files on the computer.

Because it would be impractical (and probably unwise) to observe directly how each person uses the computer, Windows NT keeps track of certain events that occur on the computer. This process, called *auditing,* creates a log of these events that you can subsequently examine to see how the computer is being used. See the section "What is auditing?" on pages 118–119 for more information.

What is auditing?

Auditing is the process by which Windows NT records various security-related events that occur on the computer. The resulting security log can be viewed with the Event Viewer. The system administrator specifies the amount and type of auditing that Windows NT is to conduct.

Security auditing is a special-purpose application of the event-logging service that records system events that affect the computer's security. You can examine the resulting log to ascertain whether a user is violating security policy (for example, by attempting to modify operating system files).

Windows NT can record a range of event types, from system-wide events (such as a user logging on) to an attempt by a particular user to read a specific file. Windows NT can record both successful and unsuccessful attempts of a user to perform actions.

Windows NT records the following information for each event:

- The date on which the event occurred

- The time at which the event occurred

- The application or operating system component that generated the event

- The type of event that occurred (for example, success or failure at performing an audited action)

- The category of event that occurred (such as file system access or logon)

- A numeric identifier for the specific event

- The username of the user who caused the event to occur

- The name of the computer on which the event occurred

- A description of the event

- "Raw" data associated with the event, when appropriate

The effect of recording this information is to create an "audit trail" that you can examine to determine how effectively your security setup is protecting your computer.

For example, if you are concerned about a virus infecting your computer's program files, you can use file permissions to ensure that only certain users can change those files (such as to upgrade them) and then set up auditing to record attempts to modify those files. When you review the security log, you can look for evidence of virus activity by looking for attempts to modify the program files. If the log contains records of such attempts by an unauthorized user, there's a good chance that a program the user ran contained a virus that attempted to propagate itself by inserting a copy of itself into the program file.

Auditing can reveal various kinds of attempts to breach the computer's security, such as letting you see whether someone has been trying to "break into" your computer by attempting to guess a password, and what that person did if he or she succeeded. Auditing can also reveal whether a user who should not have permission to gain access to certain files is actually able to do so.

Auditing is not only useful for detecting intentional efforts to compromise your system's integrity—it can also help you monitor who is using your computer and how. By tracking when a user logs on and logs off, you can determine whether the computer is being used in an economical manner.

Auditing keeps a record of important events that might affect your computer's security.

What kinds of events should I audit?

Because the security log is limited in size you must carefully choose the events you want to audit. At a minimum you should audit events that represent clear attempts to defeat security, such as failed attempts to log on or to perform actions that require special privileges. If possible, you should also audit attempts to modify program and system files and attempts to gain access to confidential files.

As audited events occur on your computer, Windows NT records the information in a security log on your computer's hard disk. Because this log is generated automatically, it's necessary to limit its size. Otherwise, the log could grow to fill all available space on the computer's hard disk. The events you choose to audit depend in part on the amount of disk space you are willing to devote to the log. If you want the log to occupy only a small amount of space, you must carefully select the events you want to audit based on your security needs and the frequency with which you expect the events to occur. If, however, you are willing to allow the log to grow to a relatively large size, you can choose to audit more events and those that occur frequently.

Choosing the types and categories of events to audit allows you a choice among supporting various levels of security. Auditing only a few critical events allows you to easily spot the most blatant attempts to bypass or defeat your computer's security. Auditing a larger number of events can help you discover more subtle efforts to compromise your computer's integrity.

The type of auditing you perform depends on the availability of your computer to people who are not authorized users as well as the importance of maintaining the integrity or privacy (or both) of your computer's data.

Minimum security requirements

If your computer is reasonably secure physically (for example, if it's not located in a public place or connected to a large network) and if you are not concerned about monitoring your computer's authorized users, you can set up auditing on your computer to record only overt attempts to violate your computer's security. At a minimum, your computer should be set up to record the following events:

- Failed attempts to log on to the computer

  Most of these events result from an authorized user incorrectly typing a username or password. Repeated failed attempts to log on to the same account within a short timespan, however, indicate a probable attempt to "break into" the computer's security.

- Both failed and successful attempts to change security policy

  Most successful events of this type are the result of legitimate administration of the computer. Nevertheless, you should watch for successful attempts performed at unusual times or attempts that violate your organization's security standards. Some failed attempts to change security policy might be caused by administrators who have unintentionally logged on to the computer with an account that does not belong to the Administrators group.

- Both failed and successful attempts to change certain system files

Attempts to change program files that are part of the operating system can indicate the presence of a virus attempting to infect the system. Operating system files with extensions such as EXE, DLL, and DRV should change only when the operating system is being updated by an administrator.

Higher-level security requirements

In addition to the minimum auditing described above and on the previous page, you should consider auditing the following events to help ensure even greater protection of your computer:

- Successful attempts to log on

Determining who logs on and when can help you detect inappropriate use of the computer. For example, suppose a user with an account belonging to the Administrators group logs on frequently with that account. That user might be jeopardizing the computer's security by failing to adhere to the principle of least privilege. (See the discussion "What is a user account?" on pages 54–55 for a discussion of the principle of least privilege.)

- Both successful and failed privileged actions

Auditing how a user employs accounts with special rights can help you enforce the implementation of your organization's security policy. It can also allow you to detect the possible effects of virus or Trojan horse programs attempting to undermine your computer's security. (See "Do I really need to use Windows NT security?" on pages 50–51 for a discussion of viruses and Trojan horse programs.)

- Attempts to gain access to certain files or printers

Depending on the degree of security necessary, you can monitor whether a user is attempting to read or change sensitive files or use restricted printers. You can monitor attempted access either by specific users or by all users.

How do I set up auditing?

Setting up auditing requires three steps:

1. With Event Viewer, set the maximum size of the security log and specify what Windows NT is to do when the security log is full.

2. With User Manager, specify the combinations of types and categories of events that you want to audit.

3. With File Manager, specify the files and users for which you want to audit access.

Auditing involves the interaction of three components of the operating system: the event-logging service, the user-account database, and the NTFS file system. When you log on to the computer as a member of the Administrators group, you can use Event Viewer, User Manager, and File Manager to determine how these components work together to provide the level of auditing that you want.

Configuring event logging

The event-logging service acts on behalf of the operating system and applications to record information about particular events. The operating system uses this service to record security-related events in a special location on the disk called the *security log*.

As with other logs, you set the maximum size of the security log to meet your particular needs. Choose a larger size if you want to audit a large number of events. Choose a smaller size if you don't expect to audit many events and you're concerned about having enough disk space available for other uses. To change the size of the security log, use the Log Settings command in Event Viewer.

You can also choose the action that Windows NT is to take when the log approaches its maximum size:

- Windows NT can overwrite event records as needed. This option, also known as "wrapping" the log, instructs Windows NT to replace the oldest event records with new event records when the log reaches its maximum size. Use this option if security is a low priority and if you check the security log frequently.

- Windows NT can overwrite event records that occurred prior to a specified number of days. Unlike wrapping the log, this action ensures that Windows NT keeps event records for a minimum number of days. Use this option if security is important and you check the security log more often than the specified minimum number of days records are to be kept. You should be sure that the size of the event log is large enough to hold all the records for the specified number of days.

- Windows NT can continue to write records to the log until it becomes full. Use this option if security is a high priority and you want to keep a record of every audited event. To ensure that newer records are not lost when the audit log becomes full, enable the Halt System when Security Event Log is Full check box in the User Manager Audit Policy dialog box. If you enable this feature, you *must* check and clear the audit log frequently. Otherwise, the system can halt unexpectedly and unsaved application data can be lost. If the security log is about to exceed its maximum size, Windows NT either presents a warning message or immediately halts the system, depending on the auditing policy set up with User Manager.

Configuring the user-account database

In addition to storing information about user accounts and groups, the user-account database also contains settings regarding the security policy of a computer. The security policy determines factors such as the minimum length of passwords and the rights assigned to each user. The user-account database also enforces the computer's auditing policy, which consists of the following aspects:

- The types and categories of events to be audited

    You can specify the categories of events (such as security policy changes or logons) and the type of events (either successful or failed) for each category to be audited. Unless at least one type of one category is enabled, auditing is disabled.

- What Windows NT is to do when the security log is full

    You can specify that the system is to halt when the security log becomes full or have Windows NT present a warning message informing the user that the security log's maximum size is nearly reached.

Configuring the file system

If the auditing policy of the computer enables auditing of file-system access, you must specify the directories or files to be audited and the users whose access to those files is to be audited. This process, which is similar to setting permissions on a file, is performed using the Security Auditing command in File Manager. You must be logged on as a member of the Administrators group to set up auditing for files. You can audit access to directories and files only on an NTFS partition.

How often should I check the security log?

The frequency with which you check the security log depends on how important security is to you, how often the computer is used and by how many people, and whether the computer is set up for external connections (such as via modem or over a network). You might want to check the security log frequently if several people often use the computer, especially if they are not supervised.

The auditing that Windows NT performs is useless unless the resulting security log is examined by someone who is familiar with the requirements of computer security and who knows how to interpret the security log.

If security is a high priority for you, you should treat the security log with the same concern that you would show for your organization's financial records. Just as the financial records of an organization should be examined by an independent account-ant, so, too, should the security records of your computer be examined by an inde-pendent auditor who can detect security violations.

If having an independent examiner check the security log is not practical, a designated administrator should check the security log regularly. To ensure that this is done, you should establish a schedule and the administrator should keep a record of when he or she actually checks the security log.

It might not be possible to create a fixed schedule at first. Determining how often to check the log requires experience. The person charged with examining the security log should do so frequently at first to get a feel for the number of events that are generated during routine use of the computer. From this information the security log examiner can determine whether he or she needs to check the log more or less frequently to adequately monitor the computer's use. This also helps determine the optimal size for the audit log and the amount of time the audit log should retain events. It will also help determine the types of events that you can realistically monitor.

In any case, you should ensure that the security log is checked often enough so that no event records go unexamined because they have been overwritten by newer entries (if that feature is enabled) or so that the event log does not become full. When the security log reaches its specified maximum size, an administrator must log on to the computer to clear the record, which is usually an inconvenience for both the person using the computer and the administrator (even if they are the same person).

If security is especially important, you should consider scheduling at least a superficial examination of the security log more often, preferably as often as once a week. (By default, Windows NT retains security log records for at least seven days before discarding them.) You should be sure the security log is checked more often if your computer faces unusual security exposure, such as from the following situations:

- Your computer is accessible via modem or by a large network of users

  This is a common source of computer security attack. If your computer is accessible in either fashion, you should watch carefully for failed attempts to gain access to files.

- Your computer is used by a large number of users

  The more users who regularly use your computer, the more difficult it is to monitor their actions directly and the more likely it is that one of them will be inclined to attempt to breach your computer's security.

- Your computer is physically accessible to the general public or other unknown individuals

  If, for example, the computer is set up as an "information kiosk" for use by people logged on with the Guest account, you should frequently check the computer to be sure that no one is attempting to log on to it with an account that has special rights. (See the discussion "When is the built-in Guest account used?" on pages 66–67 for more information.)

- Your computer contains proprietary or confidential data that might be valuable to someone else

  Even if the computer itself is physically isolated from unauthorized users, the lure of profiting from personal use of confidential information might prove irresistible even to a trusted user. Although you might consider it overly suspicious to be on guard against such data theft, it is no more unreasonable than requiring a regular audit of an organization's financial records.

Whenever the security log is to be cleared, a good practice is to save it to a file first. You can then archive the file for future reference before deleting it, if necessary.

How can an uninterruptible power supply protect my computer?

An uninterruptible power supply (UPS) protects your computer by ensuring that your computer can continue to run when the primary power supply is interrupted. This allows you or the Windows NT UPS service to shut down the computer in an orderly manner until the power is restored. Many UPS models also control the voltage reaching your computer, preventing potentially damaging voltage spikes and brownouts. Windows NT helps you configure and manage UPS models that can communicate with the operating system.

A UPS is essentially a rechargeable battery that supplies power to your computer when the power from the electric utility is cut off or drops below a certain voltage. Some UPS systems constantly supply power to the computer through this battery; other models detect a drop in the incoming voltage and instantaneously switch to the battery to supply power to your computer. Regardless of the method used, the UPS ensures that your computer's hardware is not affected by the loss of incoming power and provides you with the opportunity to ensure that the contents of your computer's memory are not lost.

Most computer users are aware of the devastation that a sudden loss of power can cause. The most obvious toll is the loss of data in the computer's dynamic memory (RAM). For example, if you opened a file and have made changes to it without saving those changes, all your work might be lost if the power to your computer were suddenly interrupted. Also, the open file you were using (as well as any other open files) could be left in an inconsistent state, making it difficult or even impossible to use in the future. (Note that the fault tolerance of the NTFS file system reduces this possibility, however.)

Even more serious is the possibility of damage to sensitive hardware. Certain electronic components are especially vulnerable to voltage that is too high or too low, even for a fraction of a second. Although your computer contains an internal power supply designed to provide the correct voltage to these components, it cannot always compensate for extreme changes.

The power supplied by electrical utilities is remarkably "dirty," or subject to extreme fluctuations in voltage. These fluctuations usually result from two types of events: brownouts and voltage spikes.

A *brownout* is an extended period of reduced voltage usually resulting from excessive demand on the utility's power supply. Sometimes this excessive demand can be widespread (citywide, for example) or localized (as with an overloaded building circuit). Brownouts can damage circuitry and mechanical equipment that rely on a constant voltage within a narrow range.

A *voltage spike* is a sudden change in voltage, either up or down. Most often these spikes result from an accident (such as the failure of a power utility transformer) or lightning striking a power line, even when miles away. Rapid increases in voltage can be particularly damaging to delicate circuits, yet they often happen so quickly that the user is not even aware of them.

In addition to providing an assured power supply, many UPS models also control the voltage of the power supplied to a computer. Even if the incoming power supply never fails, a UPS can still protect valuable computer equipment by preventing brownouts and voltage spikes from reaching it.

Windows NT makes it easy to work with many types of UPS systems. Many UPS units can communicate with your computer, which allows the UPS to inform the computer that its backup power supply has been engaged so that the computer can control the UPS.

Some uninterruptible power supplies allow you to configure them through the Control Panel's UPS dialog box. Depending on the UPS unit, you can set up the serial port the UPS uses to communicate with your computer, specify whether and how the UPS signals your computer in the event of a power failure, determine whether the Windows NT UPS service can shut down the computer in the event of a power failure, and specify other settings. The UPS service can also record when the power fails, when it is restored, and when the system was shut down as a result of a power failure. You can then examine these records using Event Viewer.

How can I use Backup to protect my computer's data?

Backup is a tool that can help you avoid losing valuable data. To use Backup effectively, however, you must establish a plan for backing up your system on a regular basis. You should decide how often you will back up your system, what files you will back up each time, and how you will protect the backup copy.

As personal computer hard disks increase in capacity, the data they hold becomes both increasingly valuable and difficult to replace. This is especially true when critical records are kept on a computer, such as financial records or a customer database.

As the value of the data contained on your computer's hard disk grows, so does the importance of backing it up. Data kept on a hard disk is vulnerable to mechanical problems on the hard disk itself, user's mistakes, and even natural disaster.

Although backing up your data can't prevent all data loss, it can minimize that loss. Instead of losing several months' worth of work, you can arrange to lose no more than a few hours' worth.

In addition to helping you recover lost or damaged data, regularly backing up your computer's files can make it easier to archive that data for legal or historical purposes. Such archiving allows you to remove older, unused files from your hard disk, safe in the knowledge that you can recover them if necessary.

To get the most benefit from backing up your computer's hard disk, you should establish a backup policy and follow it rigorously. The following are some of the considerations you should include in that policy:

- What files you back up
- How often you back up those files
- What methods you use to perform the backup
- How and where you store backup tapes

After you have established this policy, you should assign someone the responsibility for carrying it out. That person must be both reliable and trustworthy. The ability to back up and restore files also requires the ability to read and change those files (respectively).

Windows NT allows certain users to bypass normal security so that they can back up NTFS partitions. By default, a user whose accounts belong to a computer's Administrators group can back up and restore all files on the computer. When it is not practical or desirable for a system administrator to be responsible for backing up the system, you can give another user the ability to back up the system by adding the user's account to the computer's Backup Operators group.

Because logging on as a member of the Administrators or Backup Operators group gives a user the ability to read and change any file on the computer, it is essential that the person responsible for performing the backup be someone who can be trusted not to abuse that privilege. Even then, if security is important to you, your backup policy should provide for an independent review of the security audit log to ensure that backups are being performed according to policy. See "How often should I check the security log?" on pages 124–125 for more information.

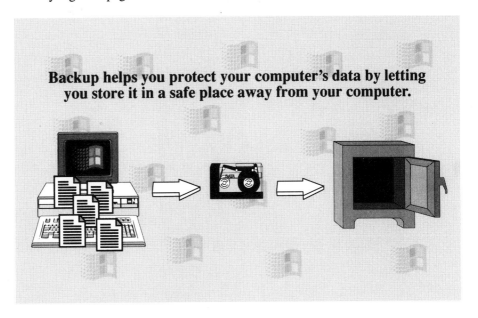

Backup helps you protect your computer's data by letting you store it in a safe place away from your computer.

What files should I back up?

You should back up any data that you have created or changed and that is important to you. You can also back up data (including application files) that you could re-create from other sources if you decide that it would be easier to restore the data from a backup tape than to re-create it.

If you had an unlimited supply of blank tapes and time, you could back up your entire disk any time you chose. But backing up all your files each time you perform a backup is rarely an efficient use of either your backup media or your time. Even when you use your computer actively, chances are that only a relatively small percentage of the files on your computer's hard disk actually change.

For example, a significant portion of your disk is taken up by operating system and application files—files that should never change (except, of course, when you upgrade them). Backing up these files each time can be a waste of both time and tape. If these files were to become lost or corrupted, you probably could restore them from the original installation disks. On the other hand, reinstalling all those program files might prove sufficiently time consuming to merit backing them up. Also, sometimes a system's setup—the unique combination of installed applications and operating system settings—might be difficult to re-create other than by restoring the appropriate files from a backup set.

Another criterion to consider when selecting files to back up is their relationship to your organization's primary purpose. In some organizations, users employ their computers for both business and personal reasons. You might want to ensure that users' personal files are kept separate from those that are essential to your organization so that the personal files are either not backed up or are backed up less regularly.

When you choose which files to back up, you should make the data files you created your highest priority. Most likely, these files represent the highest investment of your time and hence are probably the most valuable to you. Even among these files, however, you might want to distinguish between files containing data also stored elsewhere (such as in paper records) and data that would be difficult or impossible to reconstruct by other means. Certainly it is more important to back up valuable data that exists only on your computer's hard disk.

If you choose to regularly back up only data files, you will probably find that selecting those files is easier if they are stored in directories separate from program files. One method for arranging this is to require each user to store his or her data in the user's designated "home" directory. An alternative is simply to create separate directories for applications and data, creating subdirectories in each for different types of files.

Of course, the choice of which files to back up is not quite so absolute. You can back up your entire disk once, and then back up only data files the next several times you perform backups.

One way to do this automatically is to use one of three backup methods described in the section "What methods can I use to back up my computer's files?" on pages 134–135. Depending on the method you choose, you can back up all files or only files that have been changed.

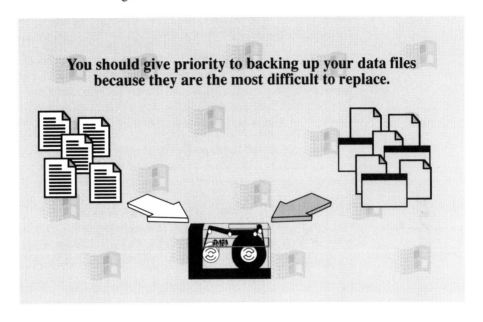

You should give priority to backing up your data files because they are the most difficult to replace.

How often should I back up my computer's files?

How often you back up your computer's files depends on how often and how much the files change and how valuable they are to you. You must balance the value of the files you back up against the value of the time required to back them up and the time required to re-create them.

Ideally, you would create a backup copy of every file you change as soon as you change it, and you would keep that copy indefinitely. Of course, backing up files immediately might not be practical—doing so could mean that you would spend about as much time backing up your files as you spend actually using them.

Instead of backing up your files constantly, you must decide how often to back them up. Although the methods you choose to perform backups affect how often you do so, there are general principles you ought to keep in mind as you decide upon a backup schedule.

The primary consideration is, of course, how actively you use the computer. There's little point in turning on a computer simply to perform a backup if the last action you performed before turning it off was a backup.

On the other hand, even occasional use can produce changes that should be backed up, especially if those changes involve data that cannot be re-created from other sources.

If the computer is used actively and for important purposes (such as for entering and processing data you need to run a business), you should back your data up frequently. You should perform some form of backup daily, if possible. Although backing up data often interferes with active use, you should consider it a worthwhile investment to interrupt the computer's regular use to be sure that its data is kept safe.

One useful guideline is to compare the time required to perform the backup against the time that would be required to re-create the data being backed up. When the time to re-create the data exceeds the amount of time necessary to back it up, you should consider performing a backup as soon as possible. In addition, if you cannot re-create the data, you should of course back up that data as soon as possible if it is important to you. (If it's not important, however, you'll probably never need to back it up.)

Other factors besides the value of the data might also affect how often and when you can back up your computer's hard disk. For example, if the storage location for your backup tapes is difficult or time consuming to access, you might have to back up your computer less often than you would like. Or perhaps the system administrator or another person designated to perform backups is available at limited times. Whatever the factors, you must take them into consideration as you develop a backup schedule.

After you develop a backup schedule, it is vital to follow it as strictly as possible. You should also let your computer's users know how often they can expect their files to be backed up so that they are aware of any time delays that might occur if sometime you must restore files from a backup tape.

The most important factor affecting the frequency of your backups is the particular method you choose each time. The sections "What methods can I use to back up my computer's files?" on pages 134–135 and "How should I decide which method to use to back up my computer's files?" on pages 136–137 will help you choose the right method to achieve the level of protection you want for your data.

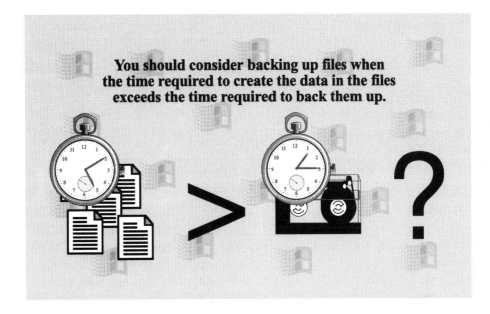

You should consider backing up files when the time required to create the data in the files exceeds the time required to back them up.

What methods can I use to back up my computer's files?

Three common methods for backing up files are

- *The* normal *method, which backs up selected files whether or not they have been changed since the last backup*

- *The* incremental *method, which backs up only selected files that have been changed since the last time you backed them up*

- *The* differential *method, which backs up only changed files but does not mark the files as having been backed up*

One of the criteria you probably want to use in selecting files to back up is whether the files have been changed since they were last backed up. Windows NT maintains a marker (called the *archive bit*) for each file, which allows backup programs to mark the files as having been backed up. When the file is changed, Windows NT marks the file as needing to be backed up again.

Backup uses the archive bit by giving you the option of backing up files you have selected only if this marker is set. You can also choose whether you want Windows NT to mark the files as having been backed up after performing the backup. The backup method you choose determines how Backup works with this marker.

When you select the normal backup method, Backup copies all selected files, regardless of the status of the archive bit, and then clears the archive bit for those files to indicate that they have been backed up. For example, if you select four files (A, B, C, and D), and files B and C have their archive bit set (indicating that they have been changed since being backed up), Backup copies all four files to the backup medium and clears the archive bit for all four files, as shown in the following illustration:

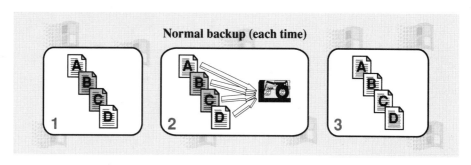

Normal backup (each time)

With the incremental backup method, Backup copies only those selected files whose archive bit is set (that is, files that have been changed since being backed up) and clears the archive bit for those files. The following illustration shows how two subsequent backups using the incremental method might work. Files B and C were changed before the first backup, and files A and C were changed between the first and the second backups:

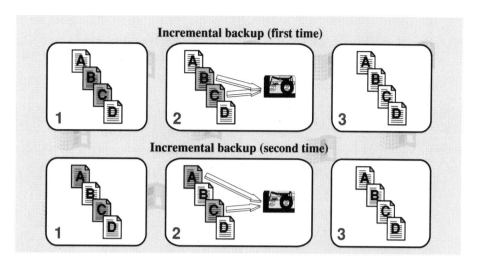

The differential method also backs up only those files that have their archive bits set. Unlike the other two methods, however, this method does not change the archive bits of files that are backed up. As a result, all files that have been changed since they were backed up using the normal or incremental method continue to be backed up in the same state until the normal or incremental method is used again to back them up. The following illustration shows two subsequent backups using the differential method. Files B and C were changed before the first backup. Between the first and second backup file A was changed:

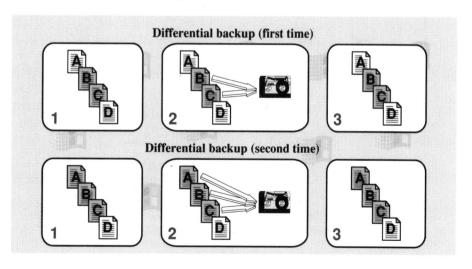

You will probably use a mixture of these three methods, depending on your particular needs. The section "How should I decide which method to use to back up my computer's files?" on pages 136–137 will help you decide how to use these methods in your backup routine.

How should I decide which method to use to back up my computer's files?

The normal method of backing up files is best when a large amount of data changes between backups, or when it's necessary to provide the baseline for the other methods. Choose the incremental method if you need to keep frequent "checkpoint" versions of changed data. Use the differential method if you want to simplify the process of restoring files. You can use a combination of the normal method plus either the incremental or differential method to provide for long-term storage with fewer tapes.

Most often, the normal method is the easiest to use: Given a set of files you have selected (often the entire disk), you know that every one of those files will be backed up. You can be assured, then, that a particular file is available on the storage tape containing the normal backup, regardless of whether the file has been changed since the previous backup. This convenience comes at a price, however. The normal method is relatively inefficient in terms of time and media because all selected files are backed up, whether or not they have been changed since the last time you backed them up—or even before that.

The normal method is the only method that allows you to take a "snapshot" of the state of a set of files (or the entire disk) at a particular time, making it especially useful for establishing a baseline for using the other two methods. Using a combination of the normal method with the incremental or differential method ensures that you can restore those files as they existed at the time you performed a particular backup.

The incremental method is, in some ways, the least convenient to use. For example, if a given file changes once during a cycle of seven incremental backups, the changed file appears in only one of the seven backup sets. Although Windows NT helps you locate the correct backup tape if you need to restore the file, you must ensure that the tape is still available. Despite this inconvenience, the incremental method is the most efficient of the three because files are backed up only when they need to be—that is, after they have changed—especially when the incremental method is used in succession for several backups.

You must use the normal method to back up the selected files before you can use the incremental method to back up the same files. After you have backed up the files with the normal method, you can then use the incremental method frequently to ensure that changed files have been backed up without using an inordinate amount of time or tape to do so.

The differential method represents the middle ground between the other two methods. Although less efficient than the incremental method, the differential method is nevertheless more convenient and safer because each subsequent backup contains all the files that have been changed since the last normal or incremental backup. If you use a combination of normal and differential backups only, you can be assured that the most recent version of a particular file is either on the tape containing the last normal backup or is on the tape containing the last differential backup.

One common strategy of backing up files requires seven tape sets and is known as the "grandparent/parent/child" strategy because it keeps at least three generations of normal backup sets. The normal backup sets must be large enough to back up your entire computer; the incremental backup sets should each be able to hold all the files that change in the course of a day.

You begin on a Friday by making a normal backup on Tape A, storing the tape on site. Then, each Monday through Thursday, you perform an incremental backup using Tapes 1 through 4, reusing these tapes each week and storing them on site as well. Each Friday you perform a normal backup and store the previous week's normal backup tape off-site. (For instance, when you use Tape B the second week, you store Tape A off site.) After you have used Tape C, you store it off-site and bring Tape A back on site for reuse.

If each tape set can hold an entire week's changes, you can use one tape set for the entire week's incremental backups, or you can use the differential method for Tapes 1 through 4. This provides additional protection because files that have been changed early in the week continue to be backed up each subsequent day.

If you need to keep permanent archive versions of files, you can choose not to reuse the tapes used for the weekly or even the daily backups, depending on how often you need to take an archival "snapshot."

How and where should I store backup tapes?

You should store backup tapes away from the computer, preferably in a vault or in another place that can protect them against fire, water, theft, and other hazards. You should store archive backups and older rollover backups in a location not likely to be affected by a disaster that might damage them.

Regardless of the backup methods you use to protect your computer's files, complete and accurate record keeping is essential if you must recover those files. Each time you perform a backup, you should record the date, tape-set numbers, and type of backup performed. If you choose to keep these records at the same site as the computer, you should also keep copies at the same location where you store your backup tapes.

Choosing an appropriate location for storing your backup tapes is critical to ensuring the safety of your computer's data. You must balance the convenience of keeping tapes near the computer against the possibility that they could be damaged by the same event that might damage your computer (such as a fire or flooding). You should store at least one generation of tapes separately from your computer, preferably in another building.

The number of tapes you store off-site depends on your purpose for storing the tape and your schedule for backing up the system. For example, if you alternate between two tape sets, making a normal backup using one set each week, you can keep the most recent week's backup with your computer (to make restoring the files easier, if necessary) and store the other week's set elsewhere. Even taking the tapes home with you (or, if you're backing up a home computer, to your workplace) serves the purpose of providing reasonable off-site storage.

If, however, your computer's files are too valuable for such an informal storage arrangement, you should consider storing your backup tapes in an off-site vault. Many cities now have businesses devoted to providing this type of protection. You might also find it economical (and perhaps more convenient) to store tapes in a bank safe-deposit box.

The location you choose for off-site storage also depends on your purpose for keeping backups. If you must keep tapes permanently for archival purposes, then you must provide safe, long-term storage. You can store the oldest of such archival tapes at the same location as your computer, but in that case you should keep them in a watertight, fireproof vault.

Except for the one or two most recent generations, tapes that could be required to restore files on your computer must be stored off-site. This includes both older rollover tape sets (tapes that are reused as part of a backup cycle) and recent archive (permanent) tape sets. It is not necessary to store rollover tape sets in a vault unless they might be affected by the same catastrophe that could damage your computer.

You should also take care to protect the tapes that you store on-site with your computer. At the very least, you should keep them away from computer monitors and other sources of magnetic fields that can damage the data on the magnetic medium. The ideal place to store them is in a small safe or strongbox that would protect them from fire or water damage.

Do not store backup tapes (other than the most recent) near the computer itself, but in a separate, safe place.

How do I restore files from a backup tape?

Backup restores files by copying them from the appropriate tape to a hard disk. If the disk partition from which the files were backed up and the disk partition to which the files are to be restored are both NTFS, access-control information can be restored along with the files themselves.

Restoring specific files to your hard disk is a relatively straightforward process, consisting of three steps:

1. Determining the files and versions of those files that are to be restored
2. Determining which backup tapes contain the desired files and versions
3. Running Backup, selecting the files from the backup tapes, and restoring the files

Of course, you will probably want to restore the most recently backed-up versions of the files to be restored, unless you need an earlier version. For example, if a file was corrupted but the corruption wasn't discovered until after the file was backed up once, you would want to restore the version immediately prior to the time the file was damaged.

Restoring a large number of files can be somewhat more complicated if you have used the differential or incremental method as part of your backup strategy. In either case, you must first restore the selected files from the most recent normal backup, then restore files from all subsequent incremental backups of those files, and finally restore the most recent differential backup performed after the last incremental backup.

For example, suppose that a directory containing many subdirectories and files was deleted. The entire disk was backed up a month ago, incremental backups of the entire disk were done the previous two Fridays, and daily differential backups were made every day this week. To be sure of getting the correct (most recent) version of all the files in that directory, you would have to restore all the subdirectories and files in that directory from the following backup sets, in this order:

1. The last normal backup
2. Both weekly incremental backups
3. Yesterday's (or, if available, today's) differential backup

When you restore to an NTFS partition files that were backed up from an NTFS partition, you can restore the original file permissions as well. You should do so only if you are restoring files to the computer from which they were originally backed up and if you want the original file permissions to remain in effect. Do not restore file permissions if you are using the backup tape to transfer files to another computer or if you are restoring files to a computer that has not been completely restored following the corruption of the operating system. Because file permissions include the unique identifier of the computer on which the files are stored, they are valid only on the original computer.

Note   You can transfer file permissions from one computer to another if both computers belong to the same Windows NT Advanced Server domain or to domains that each others' users can log on to. Only the permissions for domain user accounts will continue to be valid, however.

If the operating system on your hard disk becomes so badly damaged that your computer cannot boot, you must repair or reinstall Windows NT before restoring files backed up from the disk. If you reinstall Windows NT, you must use a repair floppy disk (which is created when Windows NT is installed on the computer) if you want to restore file permission information for the files you are restoring. The repair floppy disk ensures that the computer retains its original identifier.

P A R T 3

Using Windows NT Networking Features

What is a network?

Simply speaking, a network consists of two or more computers linked by a combination of hardware and software that lets them communicate directly. The computers use special network software to carry the data over wires or cables that link the computers.

A basic computer network is surprisingly simple, usually consisting of little more than the computers to be connected, a *network adapter card* for each computer, a special type of electrical cable to connect the network adapter cards, and the software required to allow the computers to communicate via the cards and cables.

Although all computer networks consist mainly of these basic components, the components themselves come in many varieties. A number of different network adapter cards and cables exist, and this hardware can support networks based on various topologies and protocols.

The heart of a network is the network adapter card. Usually consisting of a circuit board that plugs into a slot inside the computer, the network adapter card provides the crucial link between the computer and the network, giving the computer access to the network in much the same way that the computer gains access to its own peripheral devices such as disk drives. Special software, called a *device driver*, provides instructions the computer needs to gain access to the network adapter card and, through it, to the network itself.

Network adapter cards are connected to the cables over which they communicate according to a predefined topology. The *topology* determines how the computers are "arranged" in respect to each other on the network. The two most common topologies are the *ring*, in which each computer on the network is connected to two other computers to form a closed loop, and the *bus,* in which all computers are connected to a common communication channel.

Each topology requires its own particular method of communication among computers. One of the principal functions of this *protocol* is to establish the manner in which each computer communicates over the network.

For example, the method used in the Token Ring network, the most common form of the ring topology, requires each piece of data on the network to be built into a packet of information called a *token.* When a computer on the network receives a token, the computer determines whether the token is intended for it (in which case the computer processes the information and then sends the token on with an acknowledgment), whether the token is intended for another computer (in which case the computer passes it on unchanged), or whether the token is available for carrying data (in which case the computer might put data into the token and address the token to another computer on the network before passing it on). In the Token Ring method, network communication occurs in an orderly fashion at a relatively fixed pace.

In contrast, Ethernet, the most widely used implementation of the bus topology, appears to be much more chaotic. To send data to another computer on the network, a computer builds a packet that contains the unique identifier of the sending and receiving computers, the data to be sent, and other information. The computer then attempts to send the packet, "listening" to the network to discern whether the packet collided with a packet sent by another computer. If the sent packet did collide, the sending computer waits a random amount of time and then tries sending the packet again, repeating the process until it succeeds. Each computer on the network receives the packet and examines it to determine whether the packet was intended for that computer. If the packet is not addressed to the computer receiving the packet, the receiving computer ignores it.

Despite the apparent disorder, Ethernet is usually a better choice for small-size and medium-size networks precisely because it does allow computers to communicate directly rather than forcing them to mediate through other network computers. As a result, small-size to medium-size Ethernet networks usually have a greater total throughput than do comparably sized Token Ring networks. Ethernet networks are also usually less expensive to install and easier to manage than Token Ring networks.

Each topology and protocol has its own benefits and drawbacks. If you have not yet selected the type of network you will be using, you should consult with several computer dealers or network resellers to determine the one that would best meet your current and future requirements.

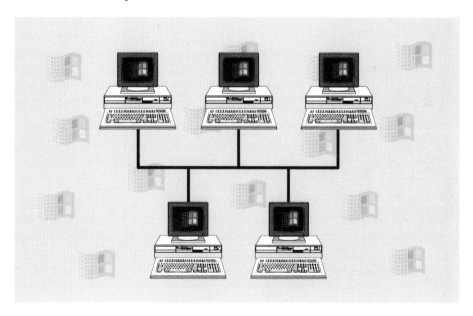

What is Windows NT networking?

Windows NT networking connects computers so that they can communicate. Every Windows NT–based computer can share its resources on a network, making the resources available to users of other Windows NT–based computers over the network. Windows NT security controls all such resource sharing, ensuring that only authorized users can gain access to sensitive resources.

The first personal computers were designed as stand-alone systems—no provision was made for personal computers to communicate with other computers. Personal computers were limited to sharing information through a process that came to be known as the "sneaker net," in which people walked from one computer to another with floppy disks containing the information they wanted to share.

Soon the limitations and problems inherent in this system became obvious, and methods emerged for connecting computers so they could communicate. Most often, these methods involved replacing or modifying the operating system of the personal computer because early PC operating systems were not capable of supporting computer-to-computer communication.

One common strategy was to replace the computer's operating system with a network operating system that could perform the same functions as the original operating system, but with additional communications capabilities. In other cases, network software was designed to run alongside the operating system while supporting the network.

Both of these solutions proved inadequate, however. Replacing the operating system meant that programs designed to work with the computer's original operating system might not work properly with the network operating system. And add-on software that ran alongside the original operating system often conflicted with other system software.

Windows NT avoids these problems by integrating network support into the operating system itself. Every aspect of the operating system, from the file system to the user interface, is designed to work with a network.

Windows NT is available in two varieties: *Windows NT* and *Windows NT Advanced Server*. Both Windows NT and Windows NT Advanced Server include all the software necessary to connect a properly equipped computer to a network, and both make it easy to share the computer's directories and files with other computers on the network, to print using network printers, and to send messages to other computers on the network. In short, built into both Windows NT and Windows NT Advanced Server is all the support necessary for establishing and managing a personal computer network.

What is the difference, then, between Windows NT and Windows NT Advanced Server? Although each comes complete with built-in network support, each supports different ways of organizing a network: By itself, Windows NT organizes a network into one or more *workgroups*, sometimes called *peer-to-peer* networks; Windows NT

Advanced Server organizes a network into one or more *domains*. Workgroups provide a simple way to set up a small network, while domains make it easier to manage a larger network. More detailed information about these types of networks and how Windows NT and Windows NT Advanced Server relate to them appears in the discussions on pages 148–153.

In addition to supporting domains, Windows NT Advanced Server provides additional features needed for larger networks. For example, Windows NT Advanced Server provides a greater degree of *fault tolerance*, the ability to continue functioning even when there is a problem with the computer hardware. Windows NT Advanced Server also includes powerful tools that make it easier to manage a large network. These features make a computer running Windows NT Advanced Server especially suited to function as a *server* on the network—a computer whose primary function is to provide services to other network computers.

Most new networks start with a small number of computers. For a small network, organizing the network into one or more workgroups is usually more appropriate. For this reason, this book concentrates on helping you set up a network organized into workgroups. Note, however, that pages 174–183 suggest how you can convert a workgroup to a domain when the need arises.

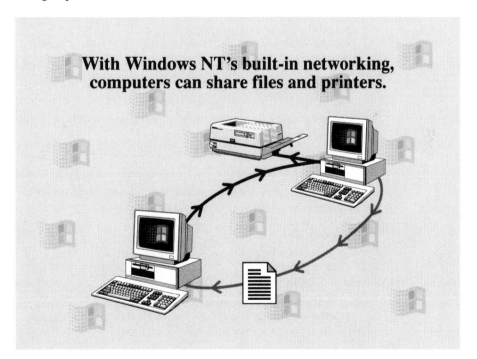

How can I use Windows NT to organize a network?

Windows NT and Windows NT Advanced Server help you organize a network in different ways. Using Windows NT, you can organize a small network into one or more workgroups in which each computer is able to share resources and use resources shared by other computers. With Windows NT Advanced Server, you can organize computers running Windows NT and Windows NT Advanced Server into one or more domains, making it easier to manage and use a larger network.

Not all networks require the same type of organization and support. Networks consisting of a limited number of computers (fewer than 20, perhaps) can typically be managed by the computers' users or perhaps by one or two experienced users who have access to each computer over the network. As computers are added to the network or as separate networks are connected, the tasks required to manage the computers on the network become more complex and time consuming, making it necesary to create a way to manage the network centrally (rather than on a computer-by-computer basis).

Windows NT lets you organize the network in a way that is appropriate for the network's size and complexity. By itself, Windows NT lets you organize the network into one or more workgroups. A *workgroup* is the simplest type of network organization to set up and manage when a small number of computers are involved. Windows NT Advanced Server, on the other hand, organizes a network into one or more domains. A *domain* makes it easier to manage larger networks because it centralizes many of the management tasks that would otherwise have to be performed individually for each computer.

The following paragraphs describe these ways of organizing a network:

Workgroups

A workgroup consists of two or more computers that can share resources such as files and printers with other computers on a network. Because computers in a workgroup relate more or less as equals, this type of network organization is often called a *peer-to-peer* network. Typically a small network is arranged in workgroups organized around departments, which makes it easier for users to gain access to resources shared by other users in their department. All Windows NT–based computers on a network belong to a workgroup unless they are members of a domain. Each computer that's a member of a workgroup must be administered separately.

Domains

A domain typically consists of several computers running Windows NT and Windows NT Advanced Server. Each computer plays a particular role in the domain. One computer runs Windows NT Advanced Server and is designated to act as the *domain controller*. The primary responsibility of the domain controller is to maintain user accounts and groups on behalf of other computers in the domain, thereby allowing users to log on to any computer in the domain using a domain user account. Other computers running Windows NT Advanced Server support the domain controller in performing these tasks and can even assume the role of domain controller if necessary.

Computers running Windows NT can belong to the domain instead of to a workgroup. A user can log on to a computer that's part of a domain with a domain user account instead of logging on with a user account meant for the computer alone. After logging on with a a domain user account, the user can gain access to shared resources on any other computer in the domain, even if the user does not have an account on that particular computer. (The user would not be able to do this if he or she logged on with a user account meant only for an individual computer.)

Security features that are centralized in the domain controller allows members of the Administrators group of the domain to administer over the network all the computers that belong to the domain.

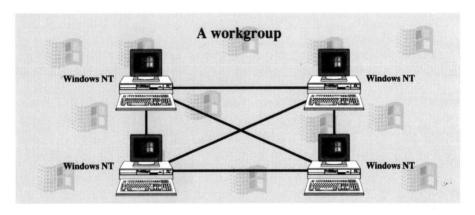

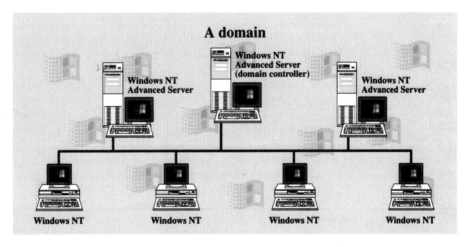

What are the advantages and disadvantages of a workgroup?

Establishing a Windows NT–based workgroup is a flexible way to organize a network because it allows users of each computer to share files, printers, and other resources. It also distributes the burden of sharing resources among several computers on the network. As they grow, workgroups are harder to manage, however, because an account must be created on each computer for each user who needs to use the computer's resources.

Generally speaking, networks organized into workgroups tend to be smaller and simpler than networks organized in other ways. Often, the first type of network an organization sets up is a workgroup that is used by a self-contained department or team that requires basic file-sharing and printer-sharing capabilities.

A workgroup is well suited to situations in which several persons have the experience and knowledge necessary to administer the computers in the workgroup. Because each computer has essentially the same role as every other computer in the workgroup, managing the workgroup is primarily a matter of individually administering each member computer.

As a result, workgroups work best in settings in which each computer has a primary user who has enough familiarity with personal computers to take responsibility for managing his or her own computer. Each user should understand how to manage files and directories on the computer, for example, and be able to use Control Panel to manage the computer's configuration.

An example of a setting appropriate for workgroups would be a small office in which each worker has a computer on his or her desk. If few enough workers are involved, it is relatively easy to ascertain that each is trained enough to manage his or her own computer.

Workgroups are less suited to situations in which computers have more than one primary user or in which most computer users are unable to administer their portion of the workgroup. In settings where the computers must be managed by someone other than the computer's principal user, a domain usually works better because the administrators of the domain can remotely manage the other Windows NT computers, taking the burden off the individual computers' primary users.

For example, a workgroup is poorly suited to settings in which two or more shifts of workers use the computers primarily for data entry, especially if each worker uses a different computer each day. Managing a workgroup used in this way would be difficult because no individual would tend to be responsible for managing one particular computer.

A further disadvantage of a workgroup is that a workgroup usually requires more computers to hold network files than does a network that has file servers set aside for the express purpose of sharing files over the network. A domain, for example, can have a few Windows NT Advanced Server–based computers with large-capacity hard disks that can be maintained as servers for network file storage, requiring Windows NT–based computers in the domain to need only enough disk capacity to hold the operating system and applications. Using domains also concentrates shared files in a few locations, making it easier for users to locate the files they need and, because of the additional fault tolerance provided by Windows NT Advanced Server, using domains also helps ensure that the files are available when needed.

Another drawback of workgroups is that workgroups with a large amount of traffic might require each computer to have a more powerful microprocessor or additional memory to avoid performance degradation when the computer's resources are used by other members of the workgroup.

What are the advantages and disadvantages of a domain?

A Windows NT Advanced Server–based domain is easier to manage centrally because the administrator of the domain defines user accounts once for the entire domain (hence for all the individual computers in the domain). In addition, domains can be set up so that a user is able to access resources in domains other than the domain in which the user's account resides. A domain might require the use of more expensive hardware and software than a workgroup, however.

A domain eliminates the need for an administrator to repeat the same tasks (such as creating user accounts) on each computer separately, which is a necessity in a workgroup. Instead, the administrator of the domain handles the administrative tasks for all computers in a domain from a computer running Windows NT Advanced Server. To add a new user to the domain, the administrator creates a domain user account that is effective throughout the domain (and in other domains "trusted" by the domain—see page 177 for more information). Because of its centralized administration, a domain is also easier for most users to work with because users do not have to supply a different password for each computer to which they connect over the network.

A domain administrator can also create and edit a profile for each user that specifies how Windows NT is to configure itself when the user logs on to any Windows NT–based computer in the domain. This gives the domain administrator a high degree of control over how each user can use the computers in the domain.

A domain provides further centralization of administrative tasks as well. Domain administrators are typically able to remotely administer computers within the domain running Windows NT or Windows NT Advanced Server because domain administrators have full administrative rights on all these computers.

Furthermore, domain administrators can set up computers running Windows NT Advanced Server to take advantage of such features as *disk mirroring* (automatically maintaining a second copy of a hard disk) and *disk striping* (creating a single logical disk volume from multiple volumes). This can help protect the integrity of network data in case of system failure.

Computers running Windows NT that belong to a domain can share their resources on the network just as they can when they belong to a workgroup. In fact, belonging to a domain makes sharing resources even easier for a computer running Windows NT because domain users do not need to have a user account on an individual computer running Windows NT to connect to it. A computer running Windows NT needs its own user accounts only for network users who do not have domain user accounts for the computer's domain or for any other domain "trusted" by the computer's domain.

The chief drawback of domains is that they usually require at least one specially trained person to maintain them. The operating system software necessary to support a domain is also more expensive, and domain controllers and servers often require more powerful (hence more expensive) hardware to support the additional demands imposed by the domain. A network large enough to require domain-based administration, however, is likely to require such advanced hardware in any case.

How can I use Windows NT to set up a network?

All the software needed to establish a simple network is an integral part of Windows NT. In addition to including software to support basic network services, Windows NT makes it easy to install network components, to manage how Windows NT works with the network, and to communicate using electronic mail and group scheduling.

Windows NT has been designed to make it easy to set up and maintain a computer network organized with workgroups. Unlike conventional operating systems, the Windows NT user interface includes built-in support for a network.

As you prepare to set up your network, you will find that Windows NT helps you each step of the way by

- Installing the network adapter card device driver

  Every computer on a network requires a network adapter card, which is the computer's physical link to the network. Special software, called a *device driver*, instructs the computer in communicating with the network adapter card. Typically the network adapter card's manufacturer supplies the device driver as well as the network adapter card. The Control Panel Network dialog box facilitates installing and configuring the correct device driver for the computer's network adapter card.

- Installing and configuring network software

  Additional software is required to allow the network adapter card to communicate with the network. This software, called *protocol software* (sometimes called *transport software*), might be supplied with the network adapter card or it might be available separately. In either case, the Control Panel Network dialog box helps you install and configure the software.

- Sharing directories and printers

  After the network hardware and software are installed, the network is ready for use. Networks are commonly employed to make directories, files, and printers available to other computers over the network. File Manager lets you share files and directories, and Print Manager lets you set up and share printers and manage network print queues.

- Connecting to shared directories, ClipBook pages, and printers

  Of course, sharing a computer's directories, ClipBook pages, and printers over the network is pointless unless other computers can easily gain access to them. File Manager and Print Manager facilitate sharing these resources.

- Controlling users' access to shared resources

  Sharing resources does not necessarily mean allowing all users unlimited access to them. Windows NT lets you control which users can connect to shared resources and how the users can employ shared resources.

User Manager lets you create user accounts that determine whether and to what degree the users can gain access to the computer's resources. These accounts also determine the degree of control users have over those resources and over the host computer itself.

File Manager lets you specify how particular users can gain access to a shared directory and, on NTFS hard-disk partitions, the shared directory's subdirectories and files as well.

Print Manager lets you specify which users can gain access to a particular printer.

- Monitoring users' access to shared resources

Complete security requires the ability to monitor user activity on the computer so that you can detect attempts to breach that security. You can set up security auditing with User Manager and File Manager, and then examine the audit logs using Event Viewer.

You can use Event Viewer to view records of other significant system events that occur on your computer as well.

- Monitoring and controlling connections to shared resources

With the Control Panel, you can determine which users are connected to your computer, list shared resources on your computer and view who is connected to them, and list files that are in use by those users. You can also disconnect any or all of those users from your computer and close files that have been opened over the network.

- Using electronic mail and group scheduling

Another important service provided by a network is its ability to facilitate communication between people. A widely used application of this type is electronic mail, which provides users with the ability to send messages from one computer to another over the network. A similar application is group scheduling, which consists of a shared appointment calendar that makes it easy to set up meetings among people who have network access. Windows NT comes complete with Mail and Schedule+ to facilitate electronic communication and meeting scheduling among network users.

Can computers running other operating systems be on the same network as Windows NT–based computers?

Appropriately equipped computers running other operating systems can operate on the same network as Windows NT–based computers if they use compatible network software and can run the same protocol to gain access to the network. (Computers can run more than one network protocol at a time.) The ability of computers running other operating systems to take advantage of some of the advanced services available on a Windows NT–based computer is limited, however.

Windows NT is designed to coexist with a broad range of computers on the same network. The networking capabilities of Windows NT are based on Microsoft LAN Manager local area network software. As a result, Windows NT is compatible with computers running LAN Manager software or similar networking software.

Personal computers running the operating systems named in the list below can share a network with Windows NT–based computers and use their resources.

- MS-DOS alone and MS-DOS in combination with Windows 3.1 (when running with software that permits access to shared resources on LAN Manager–based servers or on computers running Windows NT or Windows NT Advanced Server)
- Windows for Workgroups
- OS/2 (when equipped with LAN Manager software)

All computers sharing a network *must* be running the same network protocol. The protocol, and not the operating system, determines how computers communicate over the network. (Note, however, that the computer operating system or network operating system establishes such conventions as how resources are named and how users log on to the network.)

Computers on the same network "wire" can run more than one protocol, however, establishing what is, in effect, more than one network on the same cable. Because Windows NT supports multiple protocols simultaneously, a computer that is running Windows NT can communicate over these types of concurrent networks.

Computers running Windows NT can also gain access to resources shared by computers running other operating systems or network operating systems. For example, Windows NT can connect to computers running Windows for Workgroups, servers running LAN Manager, and servers running Novell NetWare.

The ability of computers on the network to take full advantage of the network's facilities varies depending on the capabilities of the computers' operating systems. For example, MS-DOS requires a user to assign a drive letter to a shared directory before the user can gain access to the shared directory. MS-DOS can then gain access to files contained in the shared directory (and its subdirectories) using the same naming conventions it uses for disk drives on the computer itself.

Additionally, many "network-aware" operating systems (including Windows NT) can gain access to a shared directory using the universal naming convention (UNC) method of specifying the location of a shared file on the network. A UNC pathname contains the name of the computer sharing the directory, the name of the shared directory, the path to the shared directory, and the filename itself. For example, suppose a computer named COMPUTER1 has a shared directory named PUBLIC. The shared directory contains a subdirectory named TERRYL, and a file named SCHEDULE.TXT is in that directory. The UNC pathname for that file would be \\COMPUTER1\PUBLIC\TERRYL\SCHEDULE.TXT.

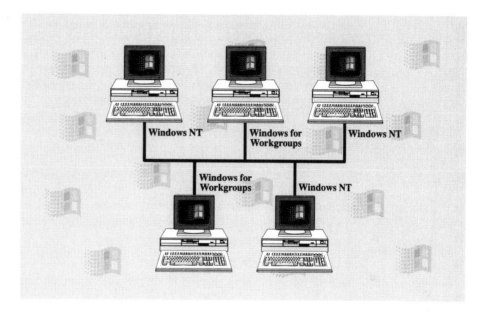

How do I plan my network?

Before you begin to set up your network, you should consider how the network will be used, who will be using it, and where its computers and printers will be located. This will help you make important decisions such as the kinds of computers you will need and where you should run the cable for the network.

Careful planning greatly simplifies the task of setting up your network. By considering in advance some important questions, such as how the network is to be used and by whom, you can be certain that the network will meet your needs. Failure to plan the network properly can not only make managing the network more difficult over the long run, but can also make expanding it difficult as your needs change.

Of course, you probably already have a good idea about how you plan to physically lay out the network. You might be putting together a network of existing computers, or you might be providing new computers to workers. Be sure that an adequate power supply is on hand for the equipment you plan to install on the network and that the network cabling can be routed so that it is out of the way and not subject to electrical interference.

Carefully planning the layout of the cable that connects the computers is especially important. Different types of network cable have different requirements concerning the maximum distance they allow between computers, for example. You should consult the manuals that accompany your network adapter cards to determine the best way to link the various parts of your network.

You will want to be sure that any new pieces of hardware you are installing (such as printers) are accessible to those who need to use them. You might also want to ensure that certain devices are *not* accessible to those who are not authorized to use them. You would not want everyone to be able to use a printer capable of printing checks, for example.

As you prepare to set up the network, you can use the following questions to guide your planning:

- Should I organize the computers into separate workgroups?

  Even if your network consists of only a small number of computers, you might want to organize the computers into separate workgroups. This can make it easier to manage the user accounts on the computers in the workgroups running Windows NT. Separate workgroups also help users to physically locate resources shared on the network by clustering computers according to their function on the network or in the organization. Note, however, that users can send Mail messages to other users and view each others' Schedule+ schedules only if the users' computers belong to the same workgroup—they cannot send messages to or view the schedules of users in other workgroups. If you plan to use these features, you should be sure that users' computers belong to the appropriate workgroups to allow them to communicate.

- How can I control who uses the network?

  Security is more difficult to implement and maintain on a network because of the ability of network users to gain remote access to other computers. By planning ahead, you can ensure that users are given access to only the computers and resources necessary for them to do their work.

- How should I train the people who will be using the network?

  Your network's users will need to know how to log on to their computers, how to connect to resources shared by other computers, how to use permissions to protect files and directories, and perhaps how to manage their own computers' shared resources. By training your users thoroughly, you can prevent future problems that might arise if users do not know how to use the network properly.

The discussions on pages 160–165 provide more detailed guidance to help you answer the questions introduced above and on the previous page.

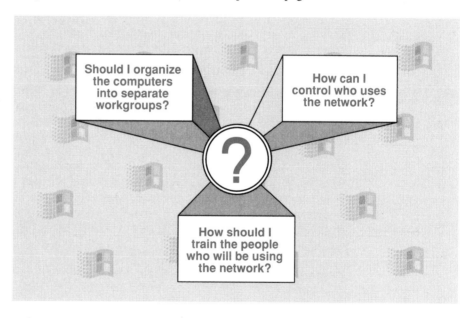

How do I organize the computers into workgroups?

If your network consists of only a handful of computers, you probably don't need to organize it into discrete workgroups. If your network includes more than 10 to 15 computers, however, you should consider dividing the computers into separate workgroups. Taking advantage of smaller, more focused workgroups will help users locate shared network resources more easily and will help you manage the user accounts on each Windows NT–based computer.

All Windows NT–based computers on a network belong either to a workgroup or to a domain. (A domain requires a computer running the Windows NT Advanced Server to be on the network. See the discussion "How can I use Windows NT to organize a network?" on pages 148–149 for more information.).

A workgroup is simply a collection of computers that all have the same workgroup name. Unlike computers in a domain, no computer that's part of a workgroup has any special role in creating or coordinating the workgroup. Instead, a workgroup is created simply by one or more networked computers declaring that they belong to the workgroup.

In addition to Windows NT–based computers, systems running Windows for Workgroups and LAN Manager can belong to a workgroup. (Note that a computer running LAN Manager joins a workgroup by specifying the workgroup name as its domain.)

A workgroup has no effect on how security works on its member computers. Every Windows NT–based computer maintains its own user accounts to let users connect to its shared resources over a network. Although a computer running Windows for Workgroups does not require users to have accounts on the computer to connect to its shared resources, it might require a user to supply a password to use a particular resource.

The way you will divide your network into separate workgroups depends on the nature of the resources you want to be readily available to each workgroup's users. Your workgroup divisions will probably be based on at least one of the following three criteria:

- Organizational divisions

    The most common method of dividing a network into separate workgroups is along departmental lines. For example, you might put the computers whose principal users work in the Human Resources department into a workgroup named HR, and you might put the computers used mostly by workers in the Accounts Receiving department into the BILLING workgroup. By making workgroup divisions correspond to departments in your organization, you make it easy for people who work together to share the files, printers, and other resources they use in the course of their daily work.

- Project teams

  Some organizations do most of their work in the form of planning and carrying out projects. Typically these projects draw upon resources—both human and material —from several departments within the organization. For example, the leader of a project charged with developing a new product might recruit workers from engineering, marketing, manufacturing, and clerical support. Even if these workers are not located in adjacent offices, they still need to share information. By placing their computers in the same workgroup, you make it easier for them to connect to each others' computers. Because users can share Mail messages and Schedule+ schedules only within their workgroup, it is especially important to include the computers used by project team members in the same workgroup to make it easier for them to communicate.

- Physical proximity

  Occasionally it makes more sense to organize workgroups according to the physical location of their member computers. For instance, if you were setting up a college library with a computer in each study carrel, it would make sense to put the computers in workgroups according to their location in the library. That way students using the computers could readily connect to shared printers on the same floor, for example. Normally, you would organize your workgroups in this way only if users do not need to share Mail messages or Schedule+ schedules.

If your workgroups will include computers running other operating systems (such as Windows for Workgroups), you might want to be sure that each workgroup contains at least one Windows NT–based computer that will be principally responsible for sharing printers and frequently accessed files over the network. Because of its ability to perform multiple tasks at the same time, a Windows NT–based computer is better able to handle the demands of the network than a computer running an operating system that can perform only one task at a time.

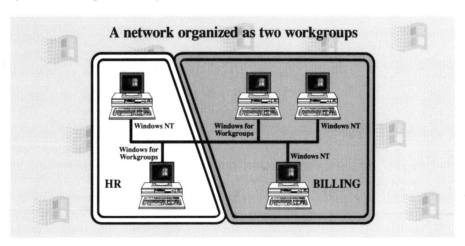

A network organized as two workgroups

How can I control who uses the network?

Windows NT security controls the use of resources on the network by controlling users' access to the Windows NT–based computers containing those resources. Users who want to log on to a Windows NT–based computer must have a user account on that computer. Normally users must also have user accounts on those Windows NT–based computers whose resources they intend to use. You can also set permissions on shared directories, files, and printers to further control how users gain access to those resources.

In a sense, anyone can use a network if he or she can use a computer connected to the network. The network itself has no control concerning who can gain access to its resources. Instead, access to resources shared by a Windows NT–based computer on the network is controlled by the Windows NT security system.

In the case of computers running Windows NT, then, the network's primary point of control is the computer that a user logs on to. If the user cannot log on to that computer, the user cannot gain access to other computers on the network. The greatest degree of network security is possible only if all computers on the network are running Windows NT, however, because otherwise an intruder might be able to try using computers running different operating systems until finding one through which he or she could gain access to the network.

Still, even if a user can log on to a Windows NT–based computer (or can use a network computer running another operating system), the user can gain access to resources on another Windows NT–based computer only if an account on the computer grants access to the user. Note, however, that computers on the network running other operating systems that can share resources (such as Windows for Workgroups) might not require individual user accounts, and might have less stringent security controls than computers running Windows NT.

You should create a user account for each person who will need access to a Windows NT–based computer. Although it might seem convenient to create accounts to be shared by more than one user, this practice hinders accountability. One of the primary purposes of user accounts is to allow you to audit how particular users are using the system. If you detect that a user is attempting to use the system in an unauthorized way, you can take corrective action. See the discussion "What is a user account?" on pages 54–55 for more information.

Windows NT provides a built-in Guest account that is typically used to allow anyone at least some level of access to the computer, most often over a network. If the Guest account is not disabled, a user without an account on the computer who attempts to connect to a shared resource on the computer automatically connects using the Guest account. (This sort of ability to connect via the Guest account makes it convenient to set up a shared directory of files that you want to make available to the general public, for example.) If you allow unknown people to use the computer through the Guest account, you should be careful to ensure that this account can gain access to the system only in a strictly controlled manner. See the discussion "When is the built-in Guest account used?" on pages 66–67 for more information.

Adequate network security requires that you control not only who uses a computer on the network, but also how they use it. Whenever you create an account to allow a user to log on to a Windows NT–based computer, User Manager automatically places that account in the Users group. You should move the account to another built-in group only if you are certain that the privileges conferred by membership in that group are suitable for the user. For example, you should assign a user an account in the Power Users group if it is appropriate for the user to share files on the network or to set up printers on the computer. See the discussion "What are built-in groups?" on pages 80–81 for more information.

In addition to controlling users' privileges on the computer, you can also control how people use the computer's resources by assigning permissions for the resources. Windows NT allows you to assign permissions that control network access to a shared directory. If that shared directory is on an NTFS partition, you can also assign additional permissions to control access to the directory, its subdirectories, and its files. See the discussion "How do I give others permission to use a file or directory?" on pages 98–99 for more information.

A common practice is to manage access to a computer's shared directories by sharing a public directory that can be freely accessed by anyone who can connect to the computer. Additional directories can be shared for the exclusive use of those who regularly connect to the computer. Project-specific or department-specific directories can also be shared with permissions that permit only the appropriate persons to gain access to them.

Computers running Windows for Workgroups can also share resources on the network. These computers have less stringent controls concerning who accesses their resources. Instead of requiring users to connect to the computer through a user account, these computers associate a password with the shared resource. Known as *share-level security*, this design enables anyone who knows the password to use the resource. Because the security on these computers is relatively lax in comparison to security with Windows NT, you should take care to ensure that these computers are not used to share sensitive resources.

Computers running LAN Manager for OS/2 can be configured to maintain user-level security (like Windows NT) or share-level security (like Windows for Workgroups). You should be certain, however, that only those computers running LAN Manager for OS/2 that are protected with user-level security are used to share sensitive resources.

How should I train the people who will be using the network?

The most important training you can provide network users concerns how to use the security features of Windows NT. Like a lock on a door, Windows NT security is effective only when it is properly used. You should also train users how to connect to shared resources and, if they are permitted to do so, how to share resources on their computers. Users having special administrative responsibilities should be taught how to perform their roles properly as well.

The type of training given each user will depend on the user's role as he or she uses a workgroup computer. Users usually fall into three categories:

- Ordinary users
- Power users
- Administrators

The category to which each person belongs depends on the level of responsibility the person will assume on the workgroup computer.

Ordinary users

An ordinary user is one who has little or no responsibility in managing computers. Instead, the ordinary user's focus is almost exclusively on using the workgroup and its computers to perform productive work rather than on maintaining the network itself.

Each user should be trained in the basics of using the operating system of the computer he or she will use. If the computer is running Windows NT, the user must know how to log on to the computer. The user also needs to learn the operating system's user interface (the means through which users control the operating system), including how to connect to and use shared network resources. The user must also be taught how to keep his or her password secret and be reminded of the importance of doing so.

Each user should understand how security is implemented on the network's computers and his or her role in relation to that security. If the user is allowed to set permissions for access to files, for example, the user should understand how Windows NT controls such access, and each user should understand the organization's policies regarding file permissions (such as whether or not administrators normally receive permission to access all files). The user should understand the importance of using groups (rather than user accounts) in permissions lists, how to create groups with User Manager, and how to assign permissions using File Manager, Print Manager, and ClipBook. For more information on user accounts, groups, permissions, and ClipBook, see Part 2 of this book.

Power users

Power users have somewhat more responsibility for managing computers and shared resources than do ordinary users. A power user (that is, a user with an account belonging to the Power Users group) is often allowed to perform some relatively simple administrative tasks, such as sharing directories and printers and creating user accounts to permit other users access to those resources.

In addition to the training given to ordinary users, power users must receive more thorough instruction in Windows NT's security features and must learn how to use these features to implement the organization's security policy. Because power users can create user accounts and share directories and printers, they must be taught how to properly use their privileges without compromising the security of computers on the network.

Administrators

Administrators are responsible for managing the computers on the network, so they commonly have total control over those computers. Typical tasks for an administrator (that is, a user with an account belonging to the Administrators group of a Windows NT–based computer) involve creating and managing user accounts and groups, controlling resource sharing, and installing and configuring software.

Because computers in a workgroup must be able to work together, administrators should have a thorough understanding of the operating systems of all the computers in the workgroup. They should be trained to diagnose and solve problems on those systems. Of course, they must also have a thorough understanding of the security features of each computer and how to use those features to implement the organization's security policies. Administrators must also understand how to bypass normal security controls when necessary.

How do I maintain the network?

Much like maintaining a mechanical device, maintaining a network serves two goals: avoiding damage and enhancing performance. Backing up data is an especially important part of preventing or being able to recover from data loss. Monitoring the network's performance and how it is being used provides the key to increasing its efficiency.

Most people are familiar with the sort of maintenance required by machines such as automobiles. An automobile's owner must change its oil frequently or risk excessive engine wear and possible breakdown. Other types of maintenance are intended not so much to prevent damage as to keep the machine running as it should—tuning up the engine, for example, to keep it operating at peak efficiency.

Although computers and other network hardware usually require little in the way of mechanical maintenance in this sense, a network does need regular attention to avoid the possibility of losing data and to ensure that the network is running as efficiently as possible. This periodic maintenance chiefly involves three activities:

■ Backing up data

  A key policy of the network administrators should be to regularly copy important data stored in shared directories to separate media so that the data can be restored if the original is lost or damaged. Windows NT provides Backup to make it easy to use the network to copy files to magnetic tape. A single Windows NT–based computer equipped with a tape drive can back up shared directories on many network computers, making it easier to protect important data on all computers belonging to a workgroup.

■ Monitoring the network

  Network administrators should periodically monitor the performance of network computers to ensure that the computers' capacity is not being underused or overused. Windows NT's Performance Monitor allows network administrators to remotely observe and record the activity of virtually any part of a computer running Windows NT. Network administrators can also use Windows NT auditing to track the frequency with which important files and directories are being accessed over the network.

■ Improving network performance

  Based on information gathered from monitoring the network, administrators should develop and implement strategies for improving system performance. Some of the methods available include upgrading system hardware and software, rescheduling certain network-intensive tasks, and redistributing shared resources on the network to avoid bottlenecks.

Of the three activities, regularly backing up data is the most important and should be performed at least several times a week. The discussions on pages 128–141 will help you formulate an effective backup policy for the computers on the network.

The other two network-maintenance tasks can be performed less often (perhaps monthly), or whenever you are concerned that network performance is showing signs of degrading.

The sections on pages 168–173 provide more information to help you develop a maintenance policy for a small network.

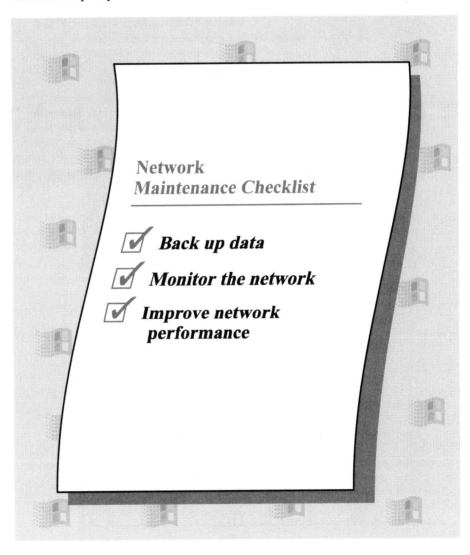

Network
Maintenance Checklist

☑ **Back up data**

☑ **Monitor the network**

☑ **Improve network performance**

When and how should I back up data on the network?

Sharing data over a network makes it even more crucial that the data be backed up frequently. You might have to establish priority levels for different kinds of data, backing up critical data more often than less important data. Although you can back up computers remotely, doing so can degrade system performance and inconvenience network users. Consider backing up computers over the network only during periods of low use.

Of all maintenance tasks, backing up the network's data is the most critical. The decreased network performance that results is usually a relatively minor inconvenience for network users—but permanent loss of important data can be catastrophic.

Backing up data is always important, even for a computer that is not part of a network. The importance of backing up data is even more urgent when the data is shared over the network, particularly if several users regularly gain access to the data. Whenever many people rely on one set of data to perform their work, the consequences of losing it are that much more severe.

Fortunately, the data is relatively easy to back up precisely because it is being shared over the network. You can back up files on all computers in a workgroup using a single tape drive installed on only one Windows NT–based computer.

To make it easier to back up files over the network, a special user account should be created on each Windows NT–based computer for the person who will be performing the backup remotely. The account on each computer should have the same username and password, and be placed in each computer's Administrators or Backup Operators group. (This allows the person performing the remote backup to gain access to files on every computer regardless of the permissions that protect the files.) The designated backup operator can then connect to each Windows NT–based computer's shared directories (or the root directory of each computer's hard disk, if a backup of the entire disk is desired) without having to supply a different username or password (or both) for each computer. (The backup operator can also back up files on directories shared on Windows for Workgroups–based computers, but the operator must supply the appropriate password for each shared directory that requires one.)

As this discussion indicates, when the files on a network computer are not backed up by the computer's primary user, a clear, well-planned, and consistently executed backup policy for the whole network makes it easier to prevent data loss. Records of the time of each backup, the files that have been backed up, the person who performed the backup, and the location of the backup media must be rigorously maintained. Because of the chance that the backup records could be damaged by the same catastrophe that could damage the computers, the backup records should also be copied, with the copies kept in a safe place.

Of course, the network's administrators and backup operators must understand and implement the backup policy. The network's users should also be familiar with the backup schedule so that they know not only how often their data is backed up, but also what data is available to be restored, if necessary.

A backup requires moving a great deal of data. As a result, the performance of the network—and particularly of the computers performing the backup and being backed up—is likely to degrade significantly. If possible, network administrators should avoid backing up a computer during the times it is most likely to be used. Many network administrators make a practice of backing up their networks during nights and weekends, when demand for the network's resources is not as great as it is during weekdays.

If backup capacity is limited, you should establish priority levels for the data to be backed up. Data that frequently changes and upon which several people rely should be backed up the most often, preferably daily. Other shared data that changes with less frequency can be backed up less often. Entire disks can be backed up even less often, perhaps on a monthly basis. Backup priority should go to computers that contain important data used by several users, although you might want to allow users to request backups for their own private data as long as doing so does not interfere with backing up data critical to your organization's primary function. For more information about Backup and related options, including practical backup plans, see the discussions on pages 128–141.

How can I monitor the network's performance and how it is being used?

Performance Monitor allows you to observe how various parts of a Windows NT–based computer are performing. Performance Monitor also provides important information about bottlenecks and other factors affecting performance. Additionally, you can use the auditing features of Windows NT to create a record of how often certain resources are accessed and by whom. This can help you determine how to distribute resources on the network for the greatest efficiency.

Although the need to maintain regular and thorough backups of network data is probably already apparent, sometimes it is more difficult to understand the need to regularly measure network performance. (Or at least the importance of such performance measuring might not become apparent until the network becomes unbearably slow or unresponsive.)

Networks usually do not experience a sudden dramatic drop in performance. Instead, as more computers are added to the network and the sheer volume of data carried by the network increases as users become increasingly dependent on it, the ability of the network to cope with the growing demand on its capacity slowly decreases.

You should take steps to detect performance degradation before it reaches the point that it becomes apparent to the network's users. Windows NT provides two tools that let you monitor how the important parts of a Windows NT–based computer are being used: Performance Monitor and auditing.

Performance Monitor is a powerful diagnostic tool that lets you observe and record virtually every significant measurable condition that exists within a Windows NT–based computer. With the regular use of Performance Monitor, you can detect changes in how a given computer is responding to the demands being placed upon it and take appropriate action.

To use Performance Monitor as a diagnostic tool, you must first establish a performance baseline with which you can compare subsequent measurements. The best time to establish the baseline is after the computer has been set up and has been in use long enough for its user(s) to be accessing its resources regularly. Note that establishing a baseline too early provides an unrealistically low measure of the demand, while recording the baseline too late might establish already degraded performance as the computer's normal performance level.

You should not attempt to record every possible item that Performance Monitor can measure—that would likely yield more data than you could possibly analyze. Instead, you should focus on those measurements that you can directly apply to a strategy for enhancing the network's performance. Examples of these measurements are cache misses, disk capacity and read/write times, processor usage, and memory fault rates.

After you have established a baseline of useful measurements, you should periodically record the same types of measurements and compare them against the baseline and subsequent measurements. With this information you can detect significant changes that might require action to improve the computer's performance.

Performance Monitor can measure system activity only on computers running Windows NT. Other tools might be available for performing similar analyses on network computers running other operating systems, however.

In conjunction with Performance Monitor, you can take advantage of the auditing facility of Windows NT and the NTFS file system to track how certain network files are being used. User Manager lets you enable file-access auditing, and File Manager lets you specify the users and files whose access you want to record. You should perform this general auditing only for a short period of time to avoid flooding the audit log with file-access events. A relatively brief sampling period should yield enough information to allow you to determine how and by whom various files are being used.

Note   If user privacy is a concern or policy of your organization, you should notify users of a computer's files that you will be monitoring their file access and why it is important for you to do so. If users object and the organization endorses their objections, you can selectively audit access by users who are willing to be monitored.

How can I improve the network's performance?

Two of the ways you can improve the performance of the network include upgrading computers on the network and distributing resources across several computers to prevent any one computer from becoming a bottleneck.

Declines in network performance are usually attributable to the capacity of a number of computers being exceeded by the demands placed upon them. Only when a network grows too large or carries a great deal of traffic does the network hardware (consisting of the network adapters and cables) itself prove to be a limiting factor.

Windows NT constantly monitors its own performance and dynamically adjusts its configuration to compensate for changing conditions. As a result, a Windows NT–based computer can usually optimize its own performance as demand upon it increases. Nevertheless, this demand can reach a point at which the capacity of the hardware itself is overwhelmed. When this happens, the computer becomes noticeably slower to its user(s).

Computer performance can usually be improved by adding additional capacity to the computer, usually in the form of upgraded hardware. The type of hardware involved depends on the type of performance to be enhanced. The following descriptions of problems are helpful for determining the kind of hardware that needs to be upgraded:

- Higher levels of cache misses

  A high percentage of cache misses is symptomatic of either a cache that is too small or a disk drive that is overactive because too many users are simultaneously accessing different files. In the former case, additional dynamic memory (RAM) might be required to allow for a larger disk cache. In the latter case, files might need to be distributed among several computers to reduce the number of users attempting to work with the files on any one particular computer.

- Decreased available disk capacity

  You can create more space on a computer's hard disk by removing files from the disk, perhaps moving them to another computer or archiving them using Backup. You can determine how to distribute the removed files to where they'll be most beneficial by using the audit log to see how they're used and who uses them. If removing files from the computer is not practical, you can install larger or additional disk drives or add more computers to the network.

- Increased read/write times

  Increased read/write times that are not the result of too many users are sometimes the result of heavy hard disk use by a few users. Examining the audit logs of the files that users access most often can suggest ways to minimize the problem, such as by distributing the files among several computers or by changing the way in which the users gain access to the files.

For example, if users are frequently saving changes to files on one particular computer, it might be more efficient for users to first move the files to their own computers, make the changes on the local copy, and then move the final version back to the file's original computer when the changes are complete.

■ Reduced microprocessor free time

A computer's microprocessor, by itself, rarely proves to be a performance bottleneck. When a microprocessor is busy, usually the disk drives and memory are working at their full capacity.

If the microprocessor itself appears to be overwhelmed, however, the culprit might be an application (such as data analysis software) that requires an unusually high amount of microprocessor time, forcing users to compete with the application for the microprocessor's attention. Such applications should be run on a computer to which fewer users will need to gain access.

If running the application on another computer is not possible or desirable, however, you might want to consider replacing the computer with a multiprocessor system. Windows NT is one of the few personal computer operating systems that can fully support computers with more than one microprocessor.

■ High rate of page faults

A high rate of page faults indicates an insufficient amount of memory, requiring Windows NT to swap data between physical memory and virtual memory (a portion of the hard disk set up to hold data as the microprocessor moves data in and out of physical memory). If possible, install additional memory in the computer. If that is not possible, you might need to consider restricting the number of users who connect to the computer.

You should also examine the system and application event logs for signs of malfunctioning hardware or software.

If network performance is inadequate even though no computers are functioning beyond capacity, it is possible that too many computers are on the network. As a result, you might have to subdivide your network, installing bridges between divisions to allow them to communicate. (A *bridge* is special hardware that links separate networks and manages the communications between them.) You might also want to consider upgrading your workgroup to a Windows NT Advanced Server–based domain to take advantage of its domain-wide administration. For more information about different types of Windows NT networks, see "How can I use Windows NT to organize a network?" on pages 148–149.

How can I upgrade a workgroup to a Windows NT Advanced Server–based domain?

A Windows NT Advanced Server–based domain facilitates managing a larger network by centralizing most administrative tasks. Upgrading a workgroup to a domain requires installing the Windows NT Advanced Server on one computer that will function as the domain controller, and then adding computers running Windows NT (and, optionally, Windows NT Advanced Server) as members of the domain.

Each computer in a workgroup is an independent entity that must be administered separately. For example, the network administrator must create user accounts on each Windows NT–based computer for every user who will be using resources on that computer. When more than a handful of computers belong to the workgroup, this separate administration becomes burdensome and can even become confusing as administrators and users try to keep track of each user's numerous accounts throughout the workgroup.

In contrast, Windows NT Advanced Server solves this problem by creating a *domain* consisting of one or more computers running Windows NT Advanced Server as well as any number of computers running Windows NT. This domain uses a centrally administered database of user accounts, located on a computer running Windows NT Advanced Server called the *domain controller*, on behalf of all the computers that belong to the domain. When a Windows NT–based computer belongs to a domain, its users usually log on to the computer using a domain user account instead of logging on with a user account on the computer itself. Users logged on with a domain user account can then connect to and use resources on any computer that belongs to the domain, even if they do not have local user accounts on those computers. In addition, domains that share the same network can be set up to "trust" each other, allowing their users to connect to computers on other domains for which the users do not have domain user accounts or local user accounts.

Windows NT Advanced Server makes it easy to use and manage such large domains because user accounts must be defined only once for all the computers in the domain. Users do not have to supply a separate password for each computer to which they connect. When a new user is added to the domain, the domain administrator creates a single domain user account with which the user can connect to any computer in the entire domain.

And even though users usually do log on to the domain, users can also continue to log on to their Windows NT–based computer directly. For example, if Windows NT–based computers continue to be administered individually by their interactive primary users, a user might log on to his or her computer with a user account belonging to the Administrators group to set up a shared directory on that computer. Such local computer accounts can also be set up to permit access to the computer for users without domain user accounts.

The first step in creating a domain is to install the Windows NT Advanced Server software on a computer that is to serve as the domain controller. The domain controller is the server with primary responsibility for allowing users to log on to the computers within the domain. Because of the extra demand placed on the domain controller, it is usually the "biggest" of all the domain's computers.

After the domain controller is set up, the domain administrator creates user accounts for everyone who will log on to any of the computers that belong to the domain, including computers running Windows NT and Windows NT Advanced Server. The domain administrator also creates appropriate global groups to make it easier to control access to network resources by large numbers of users. (A *global group* is a collection of domain user accounts that is recognized by all computers in a domain.)

When this process is complete, Windows NT–based computers can become members of the domain. Each computer's administrator or the domain administrator adds the computer to the domain using the Control Panel's Network dialog box.

When a computer running Windows NT joins a domain, the permissions given to the local accounts to protect the computer's resources continue to remain valid. Those permissions, however, are valid only when a user logs on or connects to the computer using the computer's local user accounts instead of using the domain user accounts.

Giving domain users permission to use resources shared on a computer is relatively simple if those resources were originally protected by permissions given to groups rather than to individual users. Instead of adding the domain users directly to the permissions lists protecting the resources, the domain administrator can simply replace each user's local account in the computer's groups with the user's domain user account. This one step gives the domain users permission to gain access to all the resources whose permissions lists contain these groups. The domain administrator can then delete the corresponding local user accounts, if desired. Only the domain administrator can create domain user accounts. Note, however, that the administrator of an individual computer that belongs to a domain can continue to create user accounts to provide access to that computer alone.

What is a domain?

A domain is a group of computers sharing a common database of user accounts and global groups. Because all computers in the domain share the same database of user accounts and global groups, logging on with a domain user account allows you to use files and resources on all computers in the domain.

A Windows NT Advanced Server–based domain consists of up to three principal elements:

- A domain controller

  The domain controller is a Windows NT Advanced Server-based server that maintains its database of user accounts on behalf of the entire domain.

- Other servers

  Other servers that belong to the domain can run either Windows NT Advanced Server or Microsoft LAN Manager 2.1 (or later). These computers share a single, common database of user accounts, the domain-wide database managed by the domain controller. Unlike computers running only Windows NT, these servers do not have their own database of user accounts.

- Computers running Windows NT

  Computers running Windows NT always have their own database of user accounts. When such a computer belongs to a domain, its database is supplemented by the domain user account database.

Although computers running other operating systems (such as MS-DOS or Windows for Workgroups) can connect to domain resources, they can not be members of the Windows NT Advanced Server–based domain. Nevertheless, such systems can still specify a Windows NT Advanced Server–based domain as their own workgroup or domain (depending on their operating system or network software) to simplify connecting to the domain's resources.

Every Windows NT Advanced Server–based domain has one domain controller. In fact, the presence of a domain controller establishes a domain on a network. The domain controller is responsible primarily for maintaining the user account and group information for the entire domain.

In addition to the domain controller, other servers running Windows NT Advanced Server can belong to the domain. Although these servers do not maintain the user account and group information database that the domain controller handles, they regularly receive a copy of the database from the domain controller. Having this information allows them to verify users on behalf of the domain controller, thereby avoiding an overload of the domain controller on large domains. Also, because these servers have complete, up-to-date copies of the domain controller's security information, they can be promoted to act as the domain controller if the original domain controller fails.

Although servers running LAN Manager can also be members of the domain, they cannot verify user logons in response to a request from a Windows NT–based computer, nor can they be promoted to act as the domain controller.

When a user logs on to a Windows NT–based computer with a domain user account, the computer through which the user logs on receives the user's username and password and sends it to the domain controller (or another Windows NT Advanced Server–based server in the domain). The domain controller or other server then checks the security database for an account with a matching username and password and, if it finds one, notifies the user's computer that the user has successfully logged on with the domain user account.

The server that verified the user then returns other information to the user's computer about his or her user account, including a unique number identifying the user account and all the global groups to which the user account belongs. (See pages 180–181 for a discussion of global groups.) The user's computer uses this information when checking the rights and permissions that control how the user gains access to the user's computer and to other computers in the domain.

After the user has logged on to his or her computer with a domain user account, the user can connect to shared resources on other computers that belong to the domain. If the computers are running Windows NT, Windows NT Advanced Server, or LAN Manager, the user does not have to supply a username and password for the other computers because the user has already logged on with a domain user account. Of course, for those computers that use permissions to control access to their resources, the user can access only those resources for which he or she has been given the appropriate permissions.

When two or more domains share the same network, domains can be set up to "trust" each other, enabling computers belonging to certain domains to log on those users whose accounts are in other "trusted" domains. Users can also connect to shared resources on servers that belong to domains that trust the domain in which the user has a user account. As a result, even large networks with many domains can be set up to allow a user to log on once and be able to connect to any computer on the network.

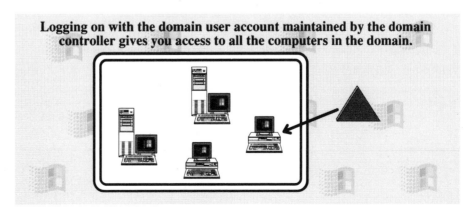

Logging on with the domain user account maintained by the domain controller gives you access to all the computers in the domain.

Can I give access to my system's resources to a user who lacks an account in my domain?

If a user does not have an account in your domain or in a domain that your domain trusts, you can still give that user access to your files or printer. Although most people who use your computer will log on using a domain user account, you can still create user accounts on your computer to allow those users without domain user accounts to connect to your computer.

Windows NT Advanced Server makes it easy to share files with the largest possible number of network users. Most often, network users will probably have an account in the domain to which your computer belongs, or they at least will have an account in a domain that your domain trusts. In this case, you can automatically share your files or printers on the network with those users via the resources' permissions lists.

Occasionally, however, you might want to allow access to a network user who does not have the necessary domain user account to enable such automatic access. For example, you might need to share a set of files with a network user who works for a division within your company that uses computers belonging to a domain that your domain does not "trust."

Fortunately, even if your computer belongs to a Windows NT Advanced Server–based domain, you can still share your computer's resources with network users the same way you would if your computer did not belong to a domain. That is, you can create an account on your computer to allow a user to gain remote access to your computer's resources, regardless of that user's domain membership. The user can then connect to shared directories and printers using the individual account that you created, rather than relying on a domain user account.

Of course, you must protect the resources you share with the appropriate permissions to allow the user to gain access to the resources. For example, suppose that you are working with Marty Lambert on a personnel report. The word processor files containing the report are kept on your computer, which belongs to the MIS domain. Because Marty does not have an account in the MIS domain (or in a domain trusted by the MIS domain), Marty cannot automatically gain access to those files using the network.

You can still give Marty access to the files, however, by creating a user account for Marty on your computer and creating a new group for the user account or adding the user account to an appropriate existing group. After you ensure that the permissions that protect the files and their directories allow the group to gain access to the files, Marty can gain access to the directories containing the files on the network.

In summary, even when your computer belongs to a Windows NT Advanced Server–based domain, you can still give users without accounts in your domain access to your system's resources in exactly the same way you would give the users access if your computer did not belong to the domain. Because the user does not have a domain user account in your computer's domain or in a trusted domain, the user does not log on with a domain user account to gain access to your computer's resources. Instead, the user connects directly to your computer by means of a user account you created on your computer for that purpose.

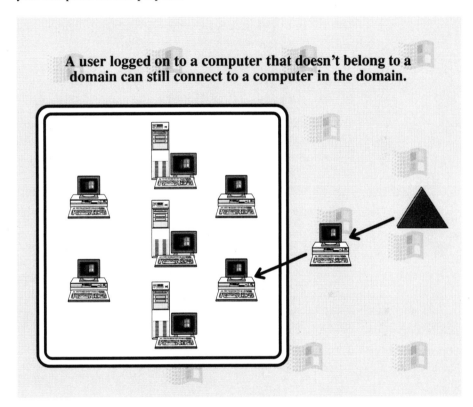

A user logged on to a computer that doesn't belong to a domain can still connect to a computer in the domain.

What are global groups?

A global group is a name that refers to several domain user accounts. Global groups can be used to protect resources on any computer in the domain as well as in other domains that trust that domain. Only the domain administrator can create global groups and add members to them.

One important feature of Windows NT security is its ability to combine user accounts into groups. Groups simplify the task of protecting system resources by making it possible in a single step to assign permissions that control access to a resource by a number of users of a particular computer.

A significant limitation of groups on a single Windows NT–based computer is that the groups are effective only on the computer containing the resource to be protected. For example, a user cannot use the same group to protect files on different computers.

Windows NT Advanced Server provides a different kind of group, called a *global group,* that is not limited to protecting a single computer's resources. A global group, which can be defined only by a domain administrator, contains a collection of domain user accounts. A global group cannot contain an account defined on a single computer running Windows NT or in a domain account from another domain. Unlike groups defined on a computer running Windows NT (called *local groups* to contrast them with global groups), global groups are available to protect resources on any computer that belongs to the domain as well as in other "trusted" domains. In other words, a domain's global groups are valid anywhere that the domain's user accounts are accepted.

When a user logs on to or connects to a computer using a domain user account, the domain reports the global groups to which the user belongs. This series of events allows a Windows NT–based computer that belongs to the domain to use the global groups to determine whether the user has permission to gain access to a particular directory, file, ClipBook page, or printer. As a result, the accounts contained in the global group must be defined in the domain in which the global group is defined; otherwise, the domain would not be able to ensure the authenticity of the user accounts in the global group.

When a Windows NT–based computer belongs to a domain, it relies on the domain to authenticate users who attempt to gain access to the computer. Therefore, the Windows NT–based computer can include domain user accounts and global groups in its local groups to protect the computer's resources. In other words, local groups on a Windows NT–based computer can contain user accounts and global groups from the domain to which the computer belongs (and any other domain trusted by the computer's domain) in addition to the computer's own user accounts.

In summary, global groups and local groups differ in the following ways:

- A local group can be used to protect files and printers only on the Windows NT–based computer where the local group is defined. In contrast, a global group can be used to protect files and printers on any computer that belongs to the domain in which the global group is defined, as well as on other domains that trust the domain.

- A Windows NT–based computer's local group can contain the computer's user accounts as well as domain user accounts and global groups from the computer's domain or from any domain trusted by the computer's domain. A global group can contain only domain user accounts from the domain in which it is defined—it cannot contain other global groups or user accounts from other domains.

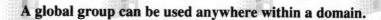

A global group can be used anywhere within a domain.

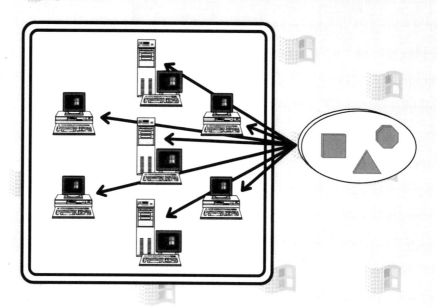

How do I use global groups?

Global groups provide a convenient way to refer to a predefined group of users within a domain. Unlike a local group, a global group can be used to protect a resource wherever it is located on any of the computers that belong to a domain. Using global groups, then, is the most convenient way to allow large numbers of users throughout the network to use a file or printer.

Global groups are used primarily for two purposes:

- Global groups are added to local groups on a Windows NT–based computer to assign special administrative privileges to a particular class of users in a domain.
- Global groups are used to control access to files and printers by a particular class of users in a domain.

For example, the Domain Administrators global group contains the domain user accounts of all users who are authorized to administer the domain. These users have the necessary privileges to manage the domain controller and servers of the domain, and by default these users also have special privileges to administer the domain's Windows NT–based computers. This is possible because when a Windows NT–based computer joins a domain, Windows NT automatically adds the Domain Administrators global group to its Administrators local group. This gives the members of the Domain Administrators global group full administrative privileges on the Windows NT–based computer.

In a similar fashion, domain administrators can use global groups to give (or deny) access permission to certain users. For example, when a Windows NT–based computer joins a domain, the Domain Users global group is added to the Users local group on the computer. This gives users who have an account in the domain the ability to gain access to files on the computer just as they would if they had accounts on the Windows NT–based computer itself.

Only a domain administrator can define new global groups and add or delete members in a global group. While at first that might seem to limit the usefulness of global groups, it actually relieves users from having to be concerned about who is a member of a global group.

For example, a domain administrator might define a global group that contains all the users in a department. As employees join or leave the department, only the domain administrator needs to make the necessary changes in the global group membership. When a user adds the global group to a local group on the user's Windows NT–based computer to grant permissions for access to resources on the computer, the user can be certain that all the employees in the department will be able to gain access to those resources.

Like domain user accounts, global groups are available to protect system resources on all computers that belong to a domain and on all computers belonging to domains that trust the domain in which the global group is defined. Users can add these global groups to local groups on their computers, making it easy to control access to their computers by many different classes of network users.

For example, one domain might contain a global group consisting of user accounts created for personnel managers in the Finance division, and another domain might have a global group containing user accounts for personnel managers in the Manufacturing division. A user can give permission to personnel managers from both divisions to gain access to files on the user's computer by creating a local group on the user's Windows NT–based computer, adding the two global groups to the local group, and then giving the appropriate file permissions to the local group. Because the membership of the global groups is controlled by the administrators of their respective domains, the appropriate people (that is, personnel managers) can continue to use the files without further action from the user, even if people are added to or removed from those groups.

Global groups, then, are most useful for controlling access to a computer's resources and for allowing remote access to a user's computer by a particular class of network users whose membership is maintained on a domain-wide basis. Users should not use global groups in these situations if they must rely on the premise of particular individuals belonging to the group—instead, the user should create a local group and add the appropriate domain user accounts for those individuals to that local group.

Appendixes

APPENDIX A

Standard and Special Permissions

Each resource has associated with it an access permission list through which the resource owner can assign access permissions to users and groups. A permission specifies the type of access (if any) that the user or members of the group are allowed for a particular resource.

A user can grant two types of permissions for controlling access to files and directories: standard permissions, which are broad permissions concerning the use of a file or directory (such as reading or changing a file), and special permissions, which are narrow permissions with which users can customize the permissions granted to a user or group. Generally speaking, standard permissions consist of combinations of special permissions.

A permission that protects a directory not only controls access to the directory itself but also can include a default file permission for the directory's files. This helps to ensure that the permissions that protect the files in a directory correspond to the permissions that protect the directory that contains the files.

The following table shows how standard file permissions consist of combinations of special file permissions.

Standard and special file permissions

	Special permission					
	Read	Write	Execute	Delete	Change Permissions	Take Ownership
Standard permission						
No Access						
Read	✔		✔			
Change	✔	✔	✔	✔		
Full Control*	✔	✔	✔	✔	✔	✔

* The Full Control standard permission provides more access than the indicated combination of special permissions. Nevertheless, there is virtually no difference between giving a user Full Control permission and all the special permissions.

The following table shows how standard directory permissions consist of combinations of special directory permissions. The last column of the table also shows the default standard file permission associated with each standard directory permission.

Standard and special directory permissions

Standard permission	Special permission						Default File Permission
	Read	Write	Execute	Delete	Change Permission	Take Ownership	
No Access							No Access
List	✔		✔				(Not specified)
Read	✔		✔				Read
Add		✔	✔				(Not specified)
Add & Read	✔	✔	✔				Read
Change	✔	✔	✔	✔			Write
Full Control*	✔	✔	✔	✔	✔	✔	Full Control

* The Full Control standard permission provides more access than the indicated combination of special permissions. Giving a user all special permissions is *not* the same as giving the user the Full Control standard permission.

The following table summarizes the types of access these special permissions provide for a file or directory.

Access provided by special permissions for files and directories

Permission	Access for a file	Access for a directory
Read	Read the file's contents (to copy or view)	List files in the directory
Write	Change the file's contents	Add files to the directory
Execute	Run a program or batch script contained in the file	Traverse the directory to gain access to files and subdirectories*
Delete	Delete or move the file	Delete or move the subdirectory
Change Permissions	Change permissions that protect the file	Change permissions that protect the directory
Take Ownership	Take ownership of the file	Take ownership of the directory

* By default, this permission has no effect because all users have the Bypass Traverse Checking right that overrides this permission. An administrator can change which users have this right.

A P P E N D I X   B

Built-In Groups

Windows NT provides a set of five built-in groups whose primary purpose is to confer different sets of privileges that determine how members of each group can control the system. A system administrator (or, to be more precise, a user logged on with an account that belongs to the Administrators group) places a user's account in one of these built-in groups to control how the user can manage the computer.

The following table summarizes the types of administrative functions that can be performed by users who are logged on with an account belonging to one of the following four built-in groups. (The Guests group is omitted because it does not confer any special administrative privileges.) If the account belongs to more than one group, the user can perform the sum of all administrative functions allowed by the groups to which the account belongs.

Built-in groups and administrative privileges

Administrative function	Users	Power Users	Backup Operators	Administrators
Save user preferences from one session to the next	✔	✔	✔	✔
Create, modify, and delete user accounts		✔		✔
Manage and delete user accounts created by others				✔
Create, manage, and delete groups	✔	✔		✔
Manage and delete groups created by other users				✔
Add and remove users in Guests, Users, and Power Users groups		✔		✔
Add and remove users in Backup Operators and Administrators groups				✔

continued

Built-in groups and administrative privileges *(continued)*

Administrative function	Users	Power Users	Backup Operators	Administrators
Assign user rights				✔
Share directories, printers, and ClipBook pages		✔		✔
Share directories as administrative shares				✔
Connect to administrative shares			✔	✔
Create, manage, share, and delete printers		✔		✔
Lock workstation	✔	✔		✔
Log off another user if workstation is locked				✔
Format hard disk				✔
Manage auditing and security log				✔
Back up all files and directories			✔	✔
Restore all files and directories			✔	✔
Set system time		✔		✔
Take ownership of files and other objects				✔

Index

Jim Groves

Jim Groves graduated from the University of Montana in 1978 with a B.A. degree in Religious Studies and from San Francisco Theological Seminary in 1982 with a Master of Divinity (M.Div.) degree. He began his second career as a technical writer in 1985 and was hired by Microsoft three years later to help write documentation for the Microsoft Windows 3.0 Software Development Kit. Since then, he has contributed to documentation for MS-DOS 5.0 as well as for Windows NT (a portion of which evolved into this book). He is married and the father of two children, Jeremy and Christy, who would never forgive him if he didn't mention their names in this, his first book.

The manuscript for this book was prepared and submitted to Microsoft Press in electronic form. Text files were formatted and processed using Microsoft Word.

Principal proofreader/copy editor: Lisa Theobald
Principal typographer: Don Hayward
Interior text designers: Mary Tjarnberg (lead), Gary Bastoky, and Lesley Jacobs
Word for Windows template: Lori Walker (lead), Microsoft Systems Division
    Technical Support Group (SysTech)
Principal illustrator: Don Hayward
Cover designer: Rebecca Geisler-Johnson
Cover color separator: Color Service, Inc.
Indexer: Shane-Armstrong Information Systems

Text composition by Microsoft Press in Times New Roman with display type in Helvetica Narrow, using Microsoft Word version 2.0 for Windows and the Linotronic 300 laser imagesetter.

In-depth References for Windows™

Programming Windows™ 3.1, 3rd ed.

Charles Petzold

"If you're going to program for Windows, buy this book. It will pay for itself in a matter of hours." **Computer Language**

The programming classic for both new Windows 3.1 programmers and owners of previous editions. It's packed with indispensable reference data, tested programming advice, keen insight, and page after page of sample programs. This edition includes one disk that contains the source code and associated files from the book.

1008 pages, softcover with one 1.44-MB 3.5-inch disk
$49.95 ($67.95 Canada)   ISBN 1-55615-395-3

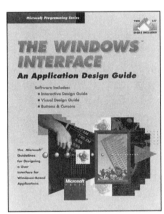

The Windows™ Interface: An Application Design Guide

Microsoft Corporation

Here is the book the developer community has been talking about, bundled with three eagerly awaited interactive reference tools. These are the Microsoft guidelines for creating well-designed visually and functionally consistent user interfaces—an essential reference for all programmers and designers working in Windows. Software includes a Visual Design Guide, an Interactive Style Guide, and cursors and buttons.

248 pages, softcover with two 1.44-MB 3.5-inch disks
$39.95 ($54.95 Canada)   ISBN 1-55615-439-9

The GUI Guide
International Terminology for the Windows™ Interface

Microsoft Corporation

This handy guide provides terminology translations and guidelines for localizing Windows-based applications for the European market. Includes translations of hundreds of GUI components—listed both by category and alphabetically—in 14 languages. The accompany disk contains all the terminology translations in both Microsoft Excel and Microsoft Windows Write formats.

256 pages, softcover with one 720-KB 3.5-inch disk
$29.95 ($39.95 Canada)   ISBN 1-55615-538-7

Microsoft® Win32™ Programmer's References

This is the official documentation for the Win32 Software Development Kit (SDK). It's the resource material that you'll need to turn to during the design and development of a Win32-based application. Volumes 1 and 2 contain overview material on systems, services, Windows management, and the Graphics Device Interface. Volumes 3 and 4 are the alphabetical Application Programming Interface (API) references. Volume 5 contains information about messages, structures, and data types.

Microsoft® Win32™ Programmer's References, Vol. 1
Systems, Services, and Windows Management
900 pages, softcover $39.95 ($53.95 Canada)   ISBN 1-55615-515-8

Microsoft® Win32™ Programmer's References, Vol. 2
Graphics Device Interface
900 pages, softcover $39.95 ($53.95 Canada)   ISBN 1-55615-516-6

Microsoft® Win32™ Programmer's Reference, Vol. 3
API Functions (A–M)
900 pages, softcover $39.95 ($53.95 Canada)   ISBN 1-55615-517-4

Microsoft® Win32™ Programmer's Reference, Vol. 4
API Functions (N–Z)
900 pages, softcover $39.95 ($53.95 Canada)   ISBN 1-55615-518-2

Microsoft® Win32™ Programmer's Reference, Vol. 5
Messages, Structures, and Data Types
900 pages, softcover $39.95 ($53.95 Canada)   ISBN 1-55615-519-0

Above titles are available June 1993

Essential Resources from Microsoft Press

Inside Windows NT™
Helen Custer
Foreword by David N. Cutler

INSIDE WINDOWS NT provides an inside look at
the design of this revolutionary operating system. Written by a member of
the Windows NT team during the system's development, this book reads like a
wide-ranging, in-depth discussion with the Windows NT developers. The author
begins with a description of the Windows NT operating system and a discussion of
the design goals, providing an overview of Windows NT and the architectural
model on which it is based, moving on to more technical topics: the NT kernel,
virtual memory manager, object management, client-server protected sub-
systems, processes and threads, future directions, and much more.
416 pages, softcover $24.95 ($32.95 Canada)   ISBN 1-55615-481-X

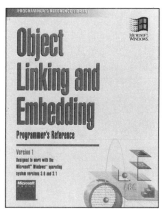

Object Linking and Embedding Programmer's Reference
Microsoft Corporation

Object Linking and Embedding (OLE) is a powerful way to extend the
functionality of your applications. This *Programmer's Reference*, critical to
programmers in developing Windows-based applications, is both a tutorial
and the application programming interface reference for OLE. The first half
of the book lays the foundation for programming with OLE, describing the
creation of OLE client and server applications. The second half offers a comprehensive and detailed reference to such topics as callback functions and data
structures, DLL functions, the registration database, and error codes.
448 pages $27.95 ($37.95 Canada)   ISBN 1-55615-539-5

The Peter Norton PC Programmer's Bible
Peter Norton, Peter Aitken, and Richard Wilton
"Admirably explains the inner workings with no loss of detail."
Computer Book Review

This is *the* ultimate reference to the IBM PC and compatible hardware and
systems software. This new edition of *The Peter Norton Programmer's Guide to
the IBM PC & PS/2,* is packed with unmatched, authoritative programming advice,
solid technical data, and key information. This book is designed to teach programmers the fundamental concepts of PC hardware, MS-DOS system calls (current
through version 6.0), essential ROM BIOS services, and graphical programming
with Windows, Windows NT, and OS/2. It's divided into four sections: PC
Hardware, PC Operating Systems, Program Development, and Reference.
608 pages, softcover $29.95 ($39.95 Canada)   ISBN 1-55615-555-7
Available May